my
mother's
diamonds

To Mary

my mother's diamonds

IN SEARCH OF THE HOLOCAUST ASSETS

James Kirby

ALLEN & UNWIN

London • Sydney

Allen & Unwin Ltd
19 Compton Terrace
London N1 2UN

First published in Australia 1998 by Prentice Hall of Australia
First published in the UK 1999 by Allen & Unwin Ltd

British Library Cataloguing-in-Publication Data
A CIP record for this book is availabe from the British Library

ISBN 1-865080-65-9

Printed and bound in Great Britain by Biddles Ltd., Guildford & King's Lynn

CONTENTS

ABOUT THE AUTHOR

Irish-born James Kirby began life as a journalist on *Business and Finance Magazine* in Dublin before moving to Australia in 1987 to join *The Australian Financial Review*.

In 1990 he moved to Hong Kong to work on *The South China Morning Post* before returning to *The Australian* in 1993. He has been a senior writer with *Business Review Weekly* since 1997.

He writes on a wide range of business issues including financial services, human resources and industry policy.

Aged 36, he is married to *The Age's* journalist Mary O'Brien and they have one child. This is his first book.

ACKNOWLEDGMENTS

First and foremost I would like to thank the people who told their stories for this book. They have a bravery and a toughness which is beyond our knowing and I hope I have not let them down.

In particular I would like to thank the following people who were instrumental in bringing the book to life.

Rabbi Itzachk Riesenberg at Yeshivah College, Melbourne, who has been the project's most enthusiastic supporter almost from its inception.

Dr Jaques Adler of Melbourne University's History department who offered his expert knowledge of Holocaust history and took the time to read the manuscript.

Jane Ogilvie at Prentice Hall Sydney who had the vision to see there was a book to be done on this subject. Also at Prentice Hall I would like to thank copy editor Bernadette Foley and production editor Esperanza Egan and editorial assistant Lisa Britt.

At *BRW* Ross Greenwood and Bob Gottliebsen who encouraged me to write and finish the book though I had been with the magazine less than a month when I announced the project.

To my friends Adrian Tame and Gideon Haigh, two seasoned authors of non-fiction work who said the right things at the right time.

I would also like to thank the following people who served as key advisors and contributors at various stages in the preparation for this book over the last two years.

In Australia, Dr Paul Bartrop (Bialik College), Dr Helen Light (Jewish Museum) Adam Ryan (Adamco), Angela Goldlust (Makor Library) Lucy Peloza (*BRW*) Matthew Stevens (*The Australian*), Pauline Rockman (Shoah Foundation) Marika Weinberger (Sydney Jewish Museum) and Elizabeth Elms who worked as a researcher on the book in its early stages.

In New York, Judith Goldberger and Irwin Nack (Holocaust Claims Processing Office). In Miami, Suzanne Hicks (University of Florida).

In Zurich, Sigi Feigel and a host of public affairs executives inside the banks who may prefer to remain anonymous in a book which will hardly improve their career prospects. In Paris, Fintan Corcoran.

In Warsaw, Konstanty Gebert (Midrasz), Marcela Kasprzyk (Australian Embassy), Peggy Simpson (Warsaw Business Journal) and Dr Slawomir Kaczorowski who acted as my guide to the city's past and present.

Two internet services must also be mentioned: the excellent Holocaust Assets site run by Geneva-based Bruno Giussani at (www.giussani.com) and the Holocaust Discussion Group at (h-holocaust@h-net.msu.edu) moderated by Jim Mott at Michigan State University.

I would also like to thank the following people who have given time and advice to the project: Henrietta Clarke, Frank Dobia, Willie Eckstein, Christian Froelicker (SBS), Abe Hoffmann, Michael Gill (*Australian Financial Review*), Bob Hawkins, Vikki Kyriakopolis (*The Bulletin*), Terence Lane (National Gallery of Victoria), Mark Leibler (Arnold Bloch Leibler), Michael Nadworny, Pinio Ringelblum, Gert Silver, Rick Vatner (*Australian Jewish News*) and Paul Wray McCann.

I owe special thanks to the Lippmann family of Melbourne and the Moen family of Perth who allowed me to quote directly from published family histories.

Due to editorial considerations a number of testimonies were not included in the final draft. However, I wish to make it very clear that every interview was a valuable addition to the process of which this book is part—the international campaign for the restitution of Holocaust era assets.

The majority of these individual stories have not before appeared in print and most of the accompanying photographs have been taken from family albums with the generous consent of those interviewed.

Finally, thank you to anyone I have failed to mention and to everyone who gave me their time.

PREFACE

This book started as a series of articles in *The Australian* newspaper in 1995 on the Swiss banks and their duties to Holocaust survivors in Australia. Since that time it has evolved into an odyssey which has taken me on a journey deep within the Jewish community in Australia and overseas.

As an outsider in that world I am forever a student, and that relationship may well have been an advantage on many occasions as survivors and their descendants often felt compelled to place their stories against a backdrop of the regional Jewish culture in which they lived.

My Mother's Diamonds began with the story of Stephen Baruch, a Polish-born Jew from the town of Lodz, and his battle to achieve a settlement with the Swiss Bank Corporation. The book ends in early August 1998 with the announcement of a global agreement between Swiss banks and Jewish activists on the issue of dormant accounts.

The signing of a global agreement on Swiss accounts, combined with the release of two key reports on the issue of Holocaust assets just weeks earlier, represents a watershed in this evolving story. Together the two events provide a natural break in a narrative which really only started with the fall of the Iron Curtain in 1989 and is set to continue well into the future.

In writing about any aspect of the Holocaust a journalist enters very difficult territory which is beyond our capacity as recorders of recent history to fully comprehend. I know that this book will upset many people both inside and outside the Jewish community. I also know that in drawing attention to the issue of financial loss in the Holocaust I may demean the greater loss the Holocaust represents. To this charge I can only offer the words of the historian Michael Marrus in his introduction to *The Holocaust in History* when he said: 'No amount of historical investigation should be permitted to detract from the awesome horror of these events, and no licence for theorising should inhibit the sense of limitation that all should have when discussing conditions that are so utterly outside our experience. Those separated from those events either by chronology or historical circumstance can never penetrate their horrors or grasp their ultimate significance.'[1]

In dealing with the issue of Holocaust survivors the wider media tends to focus on those who have 'survived' with the most success. It is natural that newspaper or television reporters concentrate on those in our society who are achievers. This means we read more often about exceptional Holocaust survivors who have built great business empires than we hear about the troubles of those who survived and put all their effort into reconstructing their lives after the unprecedented trauma of the Holocaust era.

The majority of people in this book belong to the second category; the people for whom rebuilding some semblance of a normal life was the greatest challenge.

As the debate surrounding Holocaust assets has intensified in recent years there has been a growing backlash against the move for restitution within the Jewish community. Critics have railed against what is described as a culture of complaint. The brinkmanship which is an inevitable consequence of high-level negotiations between financial institutions and Jewish pressure groups regularly prompts claims of financial greed and blackmail by Jewish interests. Worst of all, the process may be feeding biases in our own community—the myth of the rich Jew with money stashed away in a foreign place has probably been bolstered by the debate surrounding secret accounts in Switzerland.

In response all I can say is that the majority of the interviews in this book took place in modest retirement units where material wealth had clearly never been a priority. The fact that these claimants have let 50 years pass while private or public institutions grew rich on the back of their misfortune should be proof enough that we are dealing with people who are sincere in their objectives.

This book is not about money, it is about justice. It is about getting governments, banks, insurers and art galleries to do the right thing; to establish procedures for hearing claims, and to treat those claims in a fair and efficient fashion.

Time is running out for Holocaust survivors. The majority of survivor claimants in this book are now in their seventies; many of them will not be with us in ten years time. Yet their claims are still being ignored by powerful interests which continually deny or avoid responsibility.

In the final weeks of researching this book I called one last time on Arthur Shafir, a Holocaust survivor who is trying to recover funds invested by his father in an insurance policy. Shafir's claim is typical in that it commenced half a century ago in wartime Europe and has only been resurrected in recent years. He is claiming against the British multinational insurance company, Prudential Insurance.

The Sydney office of Prudential insists on sending his claim to London. Meanwhile Shafir is at a loss to even establish what procedures the group has for dealing with someone like him. Against such bureaucracy the prospect of restitution for his father's insurance policy seems remote.

As we went through the final draft of Shafir's story a television blared in another room. The embittered voice of Pauline Hanson, a radical Australian politician currently riding a wave of anti-immigration sentiment, provided a soundtrack for our interview.

As the Holocaust recedes in public memory neo-fascist groups are on the march again in every part of the world. In Australia, Pauline Hanson's public statements offer vocal evidence why the past must not be forgotten. The Hanson phenomenon proves that difficult issues such as racism, or more specifically anti-Semitism, must be dealt with effectively however unsavoury or costly in the short term.

On the eve of the Holocaust the pro-appeasement British Prime Minister Neville Chamberlain, commenting on Hitler's invasion of Czechoslovakia, talked to the British public of 'a remote place we know little about'. This dangerous attitude is with us once more in the neglect the issue of Holocaust assets has received in Australia from both the national media and all parties in government.

The losses of the Holocaust can never be replaced, but I hope this book shows that in the search for Holocaust assets it is clear that much more can be done and should be done to resolve the issue in every country.

Chapter one

SWITZERLAND,
4 MARCH 1998

It is the first day of the spring carnival in the pretty-as-a-postcard Swiss city of Basel and most office workers are still at lunch though it's now approaching three o'clock in the afternoon. This city of 300 000 retains the feel of a country town and today with a traditional parade set to roll down the main street the image of an alpine idyll seems entirely appropriate.

But as ever in Switzerland all is not quite what it seems. The standard of costume in the parade is exquisite. These revellers in medieval gowns and painted faces are not simple country folk; many are in fact bankers and stockmarket traders. Basel might look like a provincial city but it is nothing so plain. Every major European bank has interests here, and the Bank for International Settlements—the central bank for central banks—is one of the city's major buildings. You can walk around Basel in about ten minutes, but if you do it too quickly you might miss the fact that the *Wall Street Journal* can be bought at the railway station and Reuters have an office on the main street.

Just a stone's throw from the German border Basel's banking industry has enjoyed almost continued prosperity since the boom days of Swiss neutrality during World War II, when Nazis and their victims alike used this town as one big safe deposit box. Swiss Bank Corporation (SBC), Basel's biggest bank, has just announced it is to merge with Zurich-based Union Bank of Switzerland (UBS), creating the richest bank in Europe.

The merger should be good news for Basel since everyone knows the deal is really a takeover by the movers and shakers inside Swiss Bank Corporation who have long run circles round their Zurich counterparts at Union Bank of Switzerland. But the merger has hit a snag. The deeply embarrassing issue of Holocaust-era dormant accounts has loomed its ugly head yet again. In the United States the bête noire of the Swiss banking industry, Senator Alfonse D'Amato, has asked the Swiss Government to block the merger until questions regarding Holocaust-era assets at the two banks have been answered.

As the parade continues a new float turns into the main street. It's a special float devoted to Alfonse D'Amato. Beribboned with jokes at the Senator's expense the spectacle is greeted with loud applause from the crowd.

High above the parade a handful of clerical staff continue their work in the office tower of Ernst and Young. This nondescript building is the worldwide headquarters for the Swiss Bankers Association's dormant accounts project. More than 62 000 inquiries from Holocaust victims and their relatives have flooded into this office since the Holocaust assets issue exploded onto the public domain in early 1997.

At times this office has been so busy that linguistic experts were literally tripping over each other as officials struggled to deal with a myriad of claims from across the Jewish diaspora. But today the office is virtually empty. Towers of brown manila folders stand against the office walls as the sun makes a fleeting appearance over the rooftops of the city.

Inside each of these folders is a dormant account application form. The forms are all the same but not the stories behind their journey to this white-walled office. In each folder is the story of a life in the Holocaust. Applications have come from almost every country in the world; from as close as neighbouring Swiss cantons to as far away as obscure South American cities which the project clerks had to check in the office atlas.

Thomas Bauer, a partner in the Basel office of Ernst and Young which has been subcontracted to process the applications for the SBA, is genuinely concerned about the project he has taken over in recent months. A young and conscientious bureaucrat, his sincerity is palpable when he reviews the progress of the claims procedures.

'We are doing important work here and we are trying our very best to do this properly. I've always been interested in history and now I am doing something which will make history,' says Bauer.

'When I was a child I would ask my grandfather what happened during the war, but he would never talk about it, that was typical at that time. My generation is different, we want to know what happened, things are very different now.'[1]

Eight hours after it began, the carnival is in full swing. Revellers are dancing in the street and the paths of the city are littered with beer bottles. Masked musicians stumble happily across the flower beds, still playing their instruments but the precision heard this afternoon during the parade is a thing of the past. For the moment nobody cares about banks, US senators or the sins of their fathers. It is a mild night and the *fohn*—the warm spring wind that makes its way from the Mediterranean to herald the end of winter—is blowing down the streets of Basel.

Across the alps in the Swiss capital of Bern, others are enjoying themselves in a different way. Shortly after midnight there is a commotion on the front lawn of Schang Hutter's house as a group of right-wing radicals decide to pay the 63-year-old sculptor an unexpected visit.

Hutter is a controversial figure in the Swiss arts community. He won favour from the Bern authorities when he was commissioned to design a memorial to the victims of the Holocaust. He then fell foul of the same administration when he openly bickered about the exact location of his one-tonne steel memorial *shoah*. Commemorating the Holocaust is a tortuously difficult task and the saga of Hutter and his massive sculpture revealed this all too clearly. Still, the artist could never have foreseen what turn his story was about to take.

From the back of a pick-up truck Hutter's sculpture was dumped on the artist's front lawn. The far-right group later released a statement to the people of Switzerland suggesting the country had no use for Hutter's 'scrap metal' and no need to be reminded of what it represents.

4

The past will not go away for Switzerland, and the rest of the world will not leave it alone until the issue of the Holocaust assets is fully examined. It is a painful examination for a country which has long been a model of civic pride and has regularly cast a benign influence on foreign affairs. The vast majority of Swiss people did not sympathise with the Nazis during the Holocaust era. An elite within Swiss society, however, were either pro-Nazi or at the very least happy to profit from the spoils of war. These profiteers in government and the major banks were protected by the shield of Swiss neutrality.

The Swiss were not alone in benefiting from the horrors of that era. From Amsterdam to Zagreb questions are now being asked—often for the first time—about what really happened to the property and valuables held by Jewish families before the war. But any examination of the Holocaust assets affair must begin in Switzerland, it must begin on the Bahnhofstrasse; the centre of a spider's web of financial intrigue which stretched from neutral Switzerland across the financial capitals of wartime Europe.

The Bahnhofstrasse is the main boulevard in Zurich. It leads in a curved line from the magnificent nineteenth-century central railway station to the shores of Lake Zurich. Fur-coated women and cigar-smoking men still stroll the boulevard just as they have done for longer than anyone can remember. The street oozes money. Cartier diamonds, Fabergé eggs, Armani suits, and Rolex watches feature in every second shop window. In the restaurant of the Savoy Baur en Ville Hotel a main course alone could set you back 58 Swiss francs—the price of meal for two in Australia.

Fifty years ago the brand names which dot the Bahnhofstrasse were making money from misery. Bally of Switzerland, which stands accused of stealing leather from Jewish factories, is located just a few doors down from Hugo Boss, which now makes suits for the executive classes but once made uniforms for the Nazis. But few brand names have been probed more thoroughly for links with the economic machinery of Nazism than the great Swiss banks—Credit Suisse, Swiss Bank Corporation and Union Bank of Switzerland.

On the Bahnhofstrasse these banks jostle for dominance as local and international investors breeze in and out of a dozen banking chambers. On the bank windows stockmarket indices, bullion prices and foreign-exchange rates keep the same investors up to date with the international money-go-round. Inside any of these banks are discreetly dressed customers queuing to open secret accounts, while in the trading rooms gold can be bought and sold with ease. Downstairs are the safety deposit storerooms where in the middle of the day the doors are left open for busy depositors who can go about their business with the minimum of interference.

In the past these safe deposit boxes held the riches of wartime Europe. For 50 years they have been an essential tool in the accumulation of wealth from corruption and vice across the world. Tyrannical African dictators have kept the loot of nations in these vaults while drug lords from South America know there is no safer place to put blood money. More recently, members of the Russian mafia have become key customers as the families who are thriving in Moscow's frontier capitalism send their children to boarding school in Gstaad and their fortunes to the basements of the Bahnhofstrasse.

Back in the 1930s it was the Swiss Bank Corporation and Union Bank of Switzerland which dominated Swiss banking. In more recent decades the growing stature of Credit Suisse has also involved that bank in the heirless assets affair, though it was not a force in pre-war Switzerland.

For Jewish business owners throughout Europe the 1930s was a time of escalating fear. Since the earlier part of the decade it had become very clear that Jews inside Germany were being victimised and were being actively sidelined by authorities in that country. As racial segregation became a reality in Germany in 1935 with the introduction of the Nuremburg laws, Jews throughout Europe began to consider their future.

With the benefit of hindsight the desperate situation facing European Jewry now seems obvious, but it was not so at the time. Today a race incident occurring in Eastern Europe will be on the evening news in New York or Sydney within hours. In Europe prior to the Second World War Jewish citizens in rural villages would often have very little evidence of the evils of Nazism until the *Luftwaffe* were literally winging their way towards their village. Jewish families in the cities were more often aware of Nazism and fearful of its potential, but the line between fact and speculation was considerably harder to draw in the days before electronic news media.

After Hitler came to power in 1933 Jewish families began leaving Europe in large numbers. Their chosen destination was generally the United States, closely followed by the United Kingdom, Australia and South America. But not everyone wished to leave their homeland. Families in the 1930s were considerably more interdependent, especially in the Shtetls (Jewish districts) of Eastern and Central Europe.

Many Jewish families decided to make a sensible compromise; they would not quit their home towns but they would put in place defence strategies by depositing their family fortune somewhere safe. For the majority of European Jews this meant either opening a bank account in Switzerland or taking out a life insurance policy with a non-German life insurance company. The trust these financial institutions engendered was deep and implicit. Jewish families might have feared the rise of Nazis but they never expected that the great financial institutions of Europe would fail them in a time of tragedy. Nevertheless, this is exactly what happened, and it began on the Bahnhofstrasse and the streets of Basel.

Swiss bank secrecy laws had been introduced in 1934, just in time for the coming inflow of Jewish money. The laws created a banking system which was unique in the world. At that time a customer only had to visit the bank once to open a secret account and deposit money. The bankers did not ask questions. Unlike today the bankers did not even demand identification. Likewise the Swiss bank industry was a sophisticated operation but it was not nearly as exclusive in that era as it is now when these banks are looking for initial deposits of around US$500 000 before a customer is taken seriously. In the early 1930s the Swiss banks were still novices in the game of hiding people's money. They were happy to take money from almost anyone: from shopkeepers to factory owners; from Jews fearing for their lives to Nazis accumulating fortunes from corruption within the Reich.

By 1944 the heyday of the Third Reich had passed. The Wehrmacht was no longer invincible and those with an eye to the future could see a time when the Allies would beat Hitler and return Europe to peace. But in Switzerland the elite corps of bankers and bureaucrats who traded with Hitler had no intention of letting the good times come to a halt. They would trade with the Reich to the bitter end. In fact, they would even trade beyond the end of the war as recent documents have shown some Swiss were hand-picked to play a role in the 'rat runs' which spirited Nazi leaders out of Europe to the safety of Argentina and Brazil in 1945.

Money had been pouring into Switzerland throughout the war and the country of six million emerged in 1945 in considerably better shape than the victors or the vanquished in the lands outside the alps.

As the Allies swept across France and up through Italy the majority of the Swiss population drew a sigh of relief. Switzerland had defended its neutrality for five years, it had played a humanitarian role through the International Committee of the Red Cross and the implicit support of Allied intelligence networks. It would soon become a major centre for the administration of postwar reconstruction. But the bankers and bureaucrats of Basel and Zurich did not share this relief. They had more pressing problems to deal with. There was the issue of Swiss assets which had been stranded in countries invaded by the Nazis; there were the questions certain to be asked by a victorious United States concerning the purchase of gold from Nazi Germany long after Germany had run out of its own domestic reserves. Moreover there was the issue of the Jews.

Switzerland had enhanced its reputation as a centre for refugees throughout the war years, taking in more than 250 000 between 1939 and 1945. However, less than one in ten of those refugees were Jewish. In a shameful agreement in 1938 the Swiss had arranged with Germany that all German and Austrian Jews have a 'J' stamped on their passports. The 'J' stamp was nothing so much as a death warrant. At the Swiss border immigration officials could spot 'J' passport holders and refuse them entry. More than 30 000 Jews were refused entry into Switzerland in this manner.

This legislation was passed at a time when the Swiss Federal Council was aware that Jews were being persecuted in increasing numbers inside the Reich. Separately the steady stream of intelligence reports from Germany which detailed the Holocaust had stunned the rest of the world but to the well-informed bankers of Switzerland it was hardly headline news. As their contacts with the Reich had deepened during the war they had quickly realised the Jews of Europe would be decimated by the Nazis. For most Swiss citizens the confirmation of the death camps represented a human tragedy of almost inconceivable breadth, but for the cadre of bankers who spent the war at their mahogany desks it meant the substantial secret accounts built up by Jewish customers in the lead-up to the war could now be reclassified as long-term deposits.

Outside the borders of the alpine idyll the rest of Europe had been going through a nightmare for the previous six years. Six million people had died in the war—three million of that number were Jews mostly killed in the ghettos or the death camps such as Auschwitz–Birkenau where the Nazis were murdering 10 000 people a day. The culture of Europe lay in ruins, from Monte Cassino to the Warsaw Royal Palace centuries of achievement lay shattered like the pagan fantasy of the Reich itself.

For many who survived the war—sometimes as the only member of their family not to be murdered by the Nazis—an uncertain and often lonely future lay ahead. Erica Deen, now living in Perth, had hid in an attic while her family's hotel was taken by the authorities. In Romania, Sarah Goldberger, who would become an Adelaide clothing manufacturer, struggled to make ends meet on an isolated farm. In a German armaments factory Arthur Shafir—a Polish Jew posing as a Catholic—had worked as a slave labourer risking death each day. A retired carpet manufacturer, he now lives in Melbourne.

Erica Turek, now a Sydney personnel executive, had clung to her mother as they walked in the freezing snows of the Ukraine.

Inside Poland—the deep heart of the Reich killing machine—two cousins clung to life with a tenacity which astounds them even now as they enter their seventies. Ruth Crane endured no less than five camps, Siegmund Siegreich escaped one camp and fought in the forests with the Polish resistance only to be recaptured and returned to the camps again. Stephen Baruch, today an accountant in Sydney, watched his mother trade her diamonds for safe passage across the alps to Italy. Krystyna Hugon, a child of the Warsaw ghetto, hid in the village of Piastow for four years. And Hillel Perlmutter, now a Sydney store owner, walked with paper bags inside his shirt on the death march of Gros Rosen.

For them Switzerland was just a dream. Reality was the Third Reich—the scream of soldiers, the pain of hunger, the deprivation of disease. They have all survived long enough to engage the Swiss banking industry in a battle which is bigger than mere dollar values. It is a battle for justice; a battle to finally set the record straight.

Each person has their own story to tell. On this warm spring night in Basel those stories are under lock and key. But sooner or later they will be heard, breaking the silence of half a century since the Holocaust.

Chapter two

THE CASE OF
A LIFETIME

On a Thursday afternoon in October 1995, Henry Burstyner took a coffee break in his office to read the papers, in particular a report on the funds of Jewish victims of the Nazis allegedly still held by Swiss banks more than 50 years after the end of the war.

Burstyner, a 52-year-old lawyer, operates from a first-storey walk-up office in the Melbourne bayside suburb of St Kilda. A large-framed, bespectacled Polish Jew, Burstyner was a late-comer to the law; he had spent most of his early professional years as a real estate agent. In more recent times he had been making a living attending to the legal details surrounding real estate sales. It was a pleasant lifestyle but far from the bright lights. Big time lawyers kept offices in the central business district near the courts; they went to St Kilda for Sunday afternoon strolls with their families.

Burstyner read with interest the newspaper report detailing further developments in Europe and the United States on the chase for Holocaust assets. In Washington another batch of US Treasury intelligence files had been released under the 50-year secrecy rule. The files had offered remarkable detail on looting by Nazis during and after the war. What is more, the papers offered proof beyond doubt that Switzerland was a virtual finance house for the Nazis. The opening of the files had triggered an unprecedented round of protest against Switzerland and according to the newspapers it seemed the Swiss were not handling the issue very well.

Inside the United States, where the intelligence files received the most attention, it was clear the reports would trigger a major upsurge in legal action against the Swiss from Holocaust survivors. Gazing from his window at the sprinkling of shoppers and day-trippers walking along the street below him, Burstyner asked himself an obvious question: could the Swiss banks owe money to anyone out there?

St Kilda was one of the best known Jewish suburbs in Australia. Since the end of the war thousands of Jewish families had settled in the district, opening coffee houses and cake shops which in turn created a fashionable and distinctly bohemian suburb. Few Jewish families in Australia were untouched by the Holocaust and Melbourne, Australia's main industrial centre, had been a favourite destination for Polish Jews.

Morris Burstyner, Henry's father, had been a tailor in prewar Tarnov, a small city in southern Poland. He spent most of the war inside a labour camp at Jumbool in present day Kazakhstan, where he worked in a rubber factory. At Jumbool Morris Burstyner and his wife Giza had their first son Henry, who was to spend his early childhood in the labour camp as the war stretched on until 1945.

After the war the Burstyner family returned to Tarnov but like many Jewish Holocaust survivors saw no future in the devastated landscape of postwar communist Poland. They emigrated to Australia in 1949, taking a flat in the Melbourne suburb of Clifton Hill. Speaking no English Morris Burstyner left the flat the first morning and walked six miles into the city to seek out Flinders Lane, the city's rag-trade district which was a virtual home away from home for thousands of Polish Jews at that time.

Now, Henry Burstyner was considering a new line of business which would take him and his family back to their roots; back to the grim realities of wartime Europe. If Burstyner started working for Holocaust survivors he would be opening old wounds, but he would also be digging deep into his own history. The search for Holocaust assets was one legal issue where Burstyner had an edge—an expertise borne out of personal experience. The corporate lawyers of Melbourne and Sydney might have spent their boyhood playing cricket in the private schools of Australia but Burstyner had done his time in the camps.

Burstyner decided to place an advertisement in the *Australian Jewish News*, the weekly Jewish affairs newspaper edited by Sam Lipski. The advertisement called for contact with Holocaust survivors or their families who believed they had a case against the Swiss banks. The level of response from the tiny advertisement was dramatic. Letters from all over Australia began to arrive. As Burstyner recalls: 'They were mostly sad letters—"my uncle had money in a bank in Poland. Can you help me?"—that sort of thing … many cases were impossible to deal with.'[1]

Burstyner knew he was working against the odds on this issue. He had contacts across Australia and in Europe, but nothing like the network of offices that would be at the disposal of a multinational law firm. Likewise he knew the majority of inquiries coming through his door, while fascinating and often tragic in their sense of loss and betrayal, were never going to get past first base when it came to dealing with Swiss banks.

As his office hours became increasingly focused on Holocaust cases and less on the mundane but lucrative world of real estate conveyance, Burstyner knew he needed a solid case to get the business off the ground. By late November Burstyner had whittled down a handful of potentially rewarding cases from more than 400 inquiries. Then one Friday afternoon an elderly man, Stephen Baruch, and his son Andre, arrived at his office. Two hours later the three men were still talking.

A courteous and elegant man in his late sixties, Stephen Baruch was a Polish-born Jew from the city of Lodz, 'the Manchester of Poland'. Lodz had been a major centre of Polish Jewry, the city had 225 000 Jews out of a population of 665 000 at the beginning of 1939. Moreover, Lodz had flourished on the back of Poland's industrialisation in the nineteenth century. The government at that time had encouraged the growth of the textile industry in the city, and with an open border into Russia the burgeoning Polish textile trade became centralised in the city which today is still the biggest urban centre in Poland after Warsaw.

The fall of communism represented a major blow for the great textile mills of Lodz which had been making uniforms for the Russian Army for generations. In the last five years the city has been slowly regaining its place as an industrial centre through a strong technology sector. But for Polish Jews in the rag trade—the *schmutters* of New York, Chicago, Melbourne and Johannesburg— Lodz will always be remembered for its smoky textile mills which spawned a deep connection between the Jewish diaspora and the clothing trade.

The family of Stephen Baruch was part of the city's famed bourgeoisie whose art nouveau mansions rivalled the great houses of Warsaw for wealth and style. Stephen Baruch's childhood days had been spent in a townhouse built within the grounds of his family's textile factory on the outskirts of the city. In summer the family holidayed at a villa in Baruchowka, a village named after Stephen's great-grandfather.

That afternoon in St Kilda, as he retold his family's story, Stephen Baruch would leave Burstyner spellbound with his detailed memory of wartime Poland and the strength of the case he had brought to the office.

Baruch speaks with a serenity that belies the dramas his family faced during and after the war. His story is laced with a boyish humour which is always bubbling under the surface as he recalls the ironies of what must have seemed like a great adventure for a seven-year-old child:

We had always lived in Lodz for as long as I could remember, it was not a very nice city, in fact it was pretty grim. But it was a boomtown since the nineteenth century when my grandfather Salem Budzyner had arrived from the nearby village of Tomaszow.

My grandfather was quite a character. He had attended a rabbinical seminary in his teens and throughout his life he remained involved in charities. He was chairman of an orphanage in Lodz and I remember hearing that he took up an invitation to attend the opening of the Hebrew University in Jerusalem, but I don't think his old rabbinical teachers would describe him as a religious man.

He slowly and steadily built up a very strong business at the textile mill which had associated factories around the city. Salem was also a member of the Zionist Religious Party and managed to get himself elected as a member of the Polish Senate for one term in 1927. He was my maternal grandfather and really a patriarchal figure who led the family in many ways.

After the war we realised he had a wide portfolio of international investments not just in Poland. He had bought speculative industrial land in the port of Haifa in Palestine, and he had money in bank accounts in England and Switzerland. Once the war ended we were able to retrieve the funds he had deposited in England relatively easily, but the story of getting the money from Switzerland is very different.

When I was a child my father Vincent worked in one of the family factories as a managing director, it was on the edge of town and we lived in a sort of complex which included our house and the factory and a few other buildings. I was born in 1932 and I was an only child in 1939. I was a seven year old and I still had not been to school. I think children used to start school much later in those days. I had a very privileged environment, I suppose, I just remember living around my house and playing in the area. We had a football field out the back of the factory.

My mother Lala and her sister Ira were very close. Her sister had a daughter Marta who was my age. I used

to meet Marta all the time in and around Lodz. We are
now in our sixties and we both live in Sydney. We are
still very close. My grandfather had also established
the local school which was near our house, and the
plan was that I would start in the school in September
1939.

So we were in our summer house at Baruchowka one
afternoon and the Germans literally arrived in the sky
over our heads, I remember the planes swooping over
the fields. It all happened so fast. I remember gazing
up at them—it was so clear you could see the plane and
pilot inside with his goggles on. We rushed back home,
but within days my father was interned in the village,
they were making all the local men walk in big groups
on the road around the city, the idea was to block
traffic on all the routes out of Lodz.

I wonder now how we left it so late ... why we
stayed, but I can also see that it must have been very
hard to leave and you never know what is going to
happen in the future. Look at South Africa, all the
people who are there today, they face a similar
dilemma. Will it get better or will it get worse?
People can only see so far ahead.

Anyway my father comes home to find that the
Luftwaffe [the Nazi airforce] have decided to make our
house a local headquarters. There were three *Luftwaffe*
officers living in our house. They walked around in
these splendid uniforms and as a young boy I was
dazzled. Things must not have been so bad then because
they used to talk to my father in a reasonable way.
They simply said to him, 'Things are going to get very
bad here, you should go while you still have a
chance.' In a roundabout way we really owe a lot to
those officers. Shortly afterwards I remember the
family getting things together as quickly as they
could, mainly money and anything they could use in the
future.

My mother Lala had a big fur coat which she took
everywhere with her. Inside the coat she had a purse
full of diamonds. She used those diamonds to pay
people all the way across Europe as we fled the Nazis.
When she was older she used to have this joke, she
could tell you how many diamonds it took to cross any
section of Poland during the war.

16

We were in a taxi travelling at night towards Warsaw
where the idea was we could have a better chance of
survival than in Lodz. Warsaw was at least under some
form of self-administration within the general
gouvernement while Lodz was in Wartheland under direct
German occupation. Things were always going to be
tougher there. People were just beginning to realise
what was happening to the Jews, and people were very
confused. At that stage at least, many people in
Poland did not go along with the persecution the Nazis
were driving. Several times we would see people make
gestures to us which said we don't support what's
going on. Even that first night in the taxi my parents
and I were all wearing our yellow stars which the
Nazis made you put on as identification. Our taxi
driver was not a Jew, I suppose he might have been a
Catholic, when we crossed into occupied Poland he
turned to me and ripped off the star and said, 'You
can forget about that now.' It was just a gesture but
I remember it.

Inside Warsaw my parents had some friends and we were
to stay with them. I got quite a shock when we
arrived. We stayed in this dreadful old apartment
building which was quite an eye-opener for a seven-
year-old boy. There was no water and no heating, it
was cold and we were sleeping every night with all our
clothes on. There was a lot of fear in those apartment
buildings, there was always people running in the
corridors and whispering in groups, we were there to
get papers which would allow us to leave Poland.

There was, I think, a Danish consul who was willing
to be bribed to get us papers, and my mother's
diamonds were used for the first of many times. I know
now that the trip to Warsaw was all part of a wider
plan which was for the whole family to rendezvous in
Trieste in north Italy before we arranged a passage to
Palestine.

We boarded a train in Warsaw bound for Vienna. It was
all very exciting for me, I had never been anywhere
outside of Lodz. We went into this carriage and we
were joined almost immediately by a group of Nazi
officers. There was no way they knew we were Jewish,
it was all very civilised in the compartment with
everyone talking and reading. I can remember running

up and down the corridors with the Nazi officers
laughing and talking. I remember one of them lifting
me up to look out the window at the scenery. As a
child you just don't pick up on the little things, my
parents must have been terrified. Though I do remember
having this vague feeling about the officers that my
parents did not really like them.

  We arrived in Vienna and the Nazi presence was of
course very strong in the city with the Gestapo
everywhere and fascist decorations on every corner. We
went to this big hotel which had swastikas flying
outside on flagpoles. There were pictures of Hitler in
the lobby and signs everywhere saying 'No Jews
allowed'. We went up to the reception and this
concierge was standing there waving his hands at all
this Nazi stuff saying to us, 'Never mind all that, it
is only to impress the authorities'. We stayed there
for three days then we caught another train to
Trieste.

In the early years of the war Trieste in Italy was one of the best
known escape routes for Central and East European Jews. The
strategic location of the port of Trieste, the relative tolerance of the
local population to Jews, and the proximity of northern Italy to the
neighbouring countries of Poland, Hungary, Czechoslovakia, and
Germany all combined to make Trieste a haven for refugees. Yet the
city was full of dangers; fascist collaborators were capable of making
life difficult for Jews well before Italy entered the war in 1940. In
Trieste Stephen and his parents rejoined other members of the
family, including his grandfather Salem Budzyner and his
grandmother Maria, his cousins Marta and Giza and an uncle Simon.

  Though Trieste offered the prospect of a sea passage to Palestine
getting aboard one of the many vessels which plied the Mediterranean
between Italy and Palestine was never going to be easy for a family of
Polish Jews. Stephen remembers:

We arrived in Trieste and looking back at it my
grandfather Salem had a master plan for us all which
was to get travelling papers in Rome and use the city
as the departure point for Palestine. The problem was
that he had been ill, and by the time we arrived in
Italy he was very ill. In any event everyone had

managed to get to the city as planned and we settled
in different pensiones around the city. We knew at
this stage the next leg of the journey was going to
take some time.

From Italy my parents were still able to correspond
with friends back in Poland. I remember my mother was
able to send letters back to Lodz through the Red
Cross. My parents and I stayed in this old building
and I remember us going to visit Salem who was very
ill, but he reached up from the bed to give me some
money and he told me how to ask for an ice-cream in
Italian.

I suppose we were all living off money we had carried
with us in various ways. I know the diamonds were
being used at every turn to buy whatever had to be
bought to keep us going. There was a lot of discussion
about the future and then what must have been a major
disaster happened when Salem died.

We were really left there in Trieste without a
leader, everything had revolved around him. I remember
going to his funeral, it was the first funeral I was
ever at. We somehow managed to organise a full funeral
in the city, he was buried in the city graveyard. I
think from that time the mantle of being the leader of
the group fell upon my father.

Time was passing now and the winter was setting in—
Trieste can be quite cold and windy in winter. In the
afternoons I used to play on the streets with this
Italian friend, a little boy my own age, he was one of
the Barlila—the Mussolini youth brigade—he used to have
this marvellous black shirt and a toy wooden rifle that
I used to envy. After Salem's death my father went down
to Rome to get the travelling papers for Palestine, he
was in Rome the day Mussolini declared war on England.
He managed to get some travelling papers in Rome and
then he rushed back to Trieste. I don't recall how it
all worked out but everyone except my parents and I
managed to go directly to Palestine by ship.

It was decided we would make our own way to Palestine
overland as far as Athens and take a ship from there.
We were to get a train, and we went down to the
station in Trieste and ended up staying the whole
night in the station. In the morning we got on the
train which went through Belgrade and we disembarked

at Salonika in northern Greece. Salonika was an even bigger refugee centre than Trieste. There were Jewish families everywhere and kids speaking Polish on all the streets. Salonika is where I ended up having my first day at school about six months later than planned and very far from Lodz.

At that time the city was very poor but I remember everyone, Jews and non-Jews, being terrific to us; shopkeepers would pull you in off the street and give you a piece of fruit or a piece of yoghurt. I was in this French-speaking school, I think that was not uncommon in Greece at that time and we were living from day to day. But my parents would have been finding it very difficult, they were desperately trying to get to Palestine.

Then one night we packed up and we got on a train bound for Athens, we were in this little town called Larissa and there was this incredible scene at the station and the war had finally caught up with us. Italy had invaded Greece and they were bombing the train, we ran out into this railway station area in Larissa and people were running towards a bunker. We ran into this bunker which for some reason was flooded but we had no choice, we stayed there all night with water everywhere. It was terrible and I think it was the first time it got though to me that it was not all an adventure, I remember being really frightened.

But when we got to Athens everything seemed to return to normal. We had time in Athens and I remember we basically had a small holiday. It must have seemed like a complete respite from the whole odyssey for Lala and Vincent.

In Athens we finally got on a British troop ship to Alexandria. It was an amazing voyage because the weather was idyllic and the sea was deep blue and at the front of the boat there were British soldiers with rifles shooting at mines in the water, exploding them in the sea lanes before we passed through.

I was running up and down the deck watching it all with great eagerness. We had crossed the Mediterranean in these strange conditions in the summer of 1940 and the next thing I recall is being on a train near the Suez Canal, we were really close to Palestine at this stage and we were attacked again.

We were passing through this miserable little town
called Kantora and there was some sort of an air
attack. I was shouting at my parents guessing who the
planes were and trying to look at the pilots.

We ran for cover under these palm trees, it was a
really hot afternoon with nothing around but millions
of flies, and the planes sweeping over these railway
sheds shooting all round. I remember people saying,
'The planes aren't hitting anything'.

The train cannot have been badly damaged because we
got back on it again, and it travelled on to Tel Aviv.
The first night in Tel Aviv there was an air raid,
that was the third time we found ourselves in the
middle of an air attack, but I don't remember much
more after that.

In Tel Aviv the Baruch family joined the thousands of Jews flooding
in from all over Europe, and Vincent got a job in a local store. For
the next seven years the family lived in Israel but their ambition
was to leave for the new world as soon as they could obtain visas
from an overseas embassy.

In 1948 they finally got papers for New Zealand and settled in
Wellington. They were the second wing of the family to arrive in
that country from Poland. Earlier in the war another uncle of
Stephen's—Klemens Baruch—had arrived by way of Japan through
papers supplied by the Japanese consul in Vilna, Chuine Sugihara.

In New Zealand, Vincent, Lala and Stephen strove to build a new
life far from the dramas they had escaped and the culture they had
left behind. In terms of the suffering endured by others in the
Holocaust their experiences seemed almost privileged, yet they had
endured three air attacks and the total upheaval of their lives
during their dangerous seven-month trek to Israel.

Vincent Baruch was nearly 50 when they reached New Zealand.
Emotionally exhausted, he was never to fully recover.

My parents were shattered by the time we got to New Zealand.
It was an incredible change, my father especially found it
all very difficult. His own father had died when he was
fifteen, his mother died when he was at university. He had
already endured a fair few traumas. My mother who had lived
the sort of life European bourgeois ladies lived in the
1930s had to make some dramatic changes. She had been to a

finishing school in Lausanne in Switzerland, her days in Lodz had been taken up playing bridge and now here she was working in a dress factory in Wellington in the 1940s.

She used to say, 'My life is upside down, I retired when I was younger, I worked when I got older.' I think my father had a lot of problems, he had this guilt that he had survived the war while his brothers and sisters did not. There were ten in the family and only two of them were alive at the end of the war.

But I loved New Zealand, it was like some pleasant variation on nineteenth-century England; you could go to bed at night and leave your back door open. I spent most of my life there, it was only in 1988 when my wife, Jacky, got a chance to move back to her home town Sydney that I came to live in Australia.

We were always aware that there was money in Europe that was our inheritance and we had made occasional efforts to retrieve it. In the 1950s we managed to get the funds invested in London by Salem. There were some strange foreign exchange rules in those days and we ended up buying a car in Britain and importing it to New Zealand. So when I was growing up we were driving around in this car that was paid for from money deposited during the war, that must have made it stick in my mind that there was money in Europe we had a claim upon.

Marta's mother, Ira Weyland, died in Australia in 1967 during a visit to Sydney. Marta went back to Israel to deal with her estate and when she was going through her papers she came across an account statement from Swiss Bank Corporation dated 1938. It was pretty obvious to us that there was money which was ours sitting in the account. We had a statement to prove our ownership and it looked pretty simple. The following year Marta went to Europe and she brought the statement with her to Switzerland.

She went down the Bahnhofstrasse in Zurich and into the Swiss Bank Corporation offices, this was the late 1960s remember, only twenty years after the war and the Swiss were not under pressure like they are now. Anyway, she just called into the bank and explained the situation and some clerk said he would deal with it and went off with the statement. He said something along the lines of 'Don't call us, we'll call you', and that was it; she handed the statement over and never even got a copy of the account.

> Thankfully she had taken the precaution of writing the number down, if she hadn't I suppose I wouldn't be here telling my story.
>
> That was 1968, she went back to Sydney and started writing to Swiss Bank Corporation and they wrote back saying that they had no idea who she was, or what she was talking about. That seemed like the end of it until one day in 1995 I was in Melbourne visiting my son Andre and we saw this article in *The Australian* concerning Jewish claimants who believed they had Holocaust-era claims against the Swiss banks. We took a chance and drove over to meet this lawyer Henry Burstyner and then things started to happen.[2]

Discussing the case that afternoon in the St Kilda office, Henry Burstyner and Stephen Baruch quickly developed an understanding. They were both Polish Jews, and though they came from different sides of the tracks within Poland's class-ridden prewar society, they were united with a common grievance—a sense that justice had been denied. Now there was a chance to right the wrongs of an earlier time.

It was decided the case would be taken jointly by Stephen and Marta. Despite her best intentions Marta had made a major error in handing over the account statement to the SBC officials in 1968. As it turned out, the bank was never to return the statement. Marta had been among a tiny minority of Holocaust survivors with documentation to support a claim against a Holocaust-era account; now that crucial account statement was out of her hands.

Stephen Baruch gave Burstyner the SBC account number and told him that the account contained more than 200 pounds sterling in 1938. After weeks of trawling through many hopeless cases often with little more than a scintilla of detail, it took Burstyner a few minutes to digest just how powerful the case in front of him was: 'Then it hit me, it was a terrific case, it was the case of a lifetime,' Burstyner said.

In attracting a batch of credible cases from Australia's Jewish community Burstyner has already won the first round of the legal battle against the Swiss. He had outwitted the major law firms that would have relished the prospect of taking on the Swiss banks in an international case which had every chance of propelling the key players to celebrity status. Now Burstyner had to prove he was up

23

to the task. Despite his enthusiasm and his suitability for the case he was operating outside his sphere of influence.

Working against the tyranny of distance Burstyner began to make initial overtures in Switzerland. He contacted 24 law firms in Zurich asking if they would work with him in building a case against SBC. As Burstyner recalls, 22 firms responded with a flat refusal on the grounds they had regular dealings with Swiss banks; the remaining two offered to help for an unrealistic up-front fee of US$10 000.

An impulsive and energetic character by nature, Burstyner decided to book an exploratory trip to Switzerland. He would visit the banks in person and see for himself the world he was dealing with.

Not for the first time in this case fate was to intervene. On the plane to Zurich in November 1995 Burstyner struck up conversation with a fellow traveller, a diamond trader on his way back to Europe. The Antwerp diamond dealer told Burstyner the lawyer to know in Zurich was a certain Siegmund Feigel. Burstyner made note of the name and promised to follow up the lead when he got to Switzerland.

Unknown to Burstyner at that time, Sigi Feigel is one of the most eminent Jews in Switzerland. The honorary president of the Jewish community in Zurich, he has emerged as a vocal and intensely diplomatic figure in his trenchant support for Swiss Jews in the debate over Holocaust assets. His position as both a prominent Swiss citizen and a leading Jewish activist has seen him clash more than once with the New York-based World Jewish Congress (WJC).

In 1995 Feigel was open to any initiatives that might rouse the international media to Switzerland's hypocrisy over the treatment of the Jews during the Nazi era. He would be of crucial assistance in guiding the Melbourne lawyer through the labyrinth of Swiss bureaucracy. Moreover, he would ultimately accompany Burstyner on his visits to the SBC offices on the Bahnhofstrasse, a gesture which immediately gave the Baruch case top priority inside the bank.

Despite the sensitive nature of the Baruch case and the growing clamour surrounding Holocaust-era assets held in Switzerland, SBC in 1996 was as arrogant as 30 years previously when Marta Weyland was summarily dismissed by busy bank clerks. On Burstyner's first visit to the bank he received a cool reception from SBC officials. He was advised to forget the whole affair, the bank had little information concerning his Australian case. Firmly but politely he was told he was wasting his time. Depressed but defiant Burstyner returned to Melbourne promising himself that the next time he went to Zurich he would not be so easy to deter.

The campaign to reveal the secrets of Swiss banks gained momentum in February 1996 when the Swiss Bankers Association took its first faltering steps towards improving its public image by publicly dealing with the issue of heirless assets. In a report which now appears dramatically incomplete the SBA said there were just 775 dormant accounts with a total value of 38.7 million Swiss francs.

Jewish groups around the world, including those in Australia, were deeply suspicious of the estimates. That suspicion turned to indignation a fortnight later on 23 February as the President of Union Bank of Switzerland, Robert Studer, inflamed the situation describing the amount of heirless assets as 'peanuts'.[3]

Studer could not have done more damage to the Swiss banks' reputation if he tried. Two months later in New York, Republican Senator Alfonse D'Amato began the first of the hearings held under the auspices of the Banking Commission of the US Senate. As one Holocaust claimant after another took the stand to tell their grim stories of loss and betrayal, Studer and his fellow bankers started to look like heartless bureaucrats, the gnomes of Zurich became the poison dwarfs of international finance.

By mid May 1996 the SBA was facing a new challenge in the form of the all-powerful World Jewish Congress; as it began to accelerate the campaign against Swiss banks, the issue was also getting increased coverage in the media.

In Melbourne Burstyner spent most of 1996 balancing the business of making a living from conveyancing real estate with the considerably more challenging demands of running Holocaust claims. As the months passed he realised the public relations battle between the Swiss banks and Holocaust claimants was starting to turn in the claimants' favour. Across Australia media agencies were also beginning to take an interest in the Baruch case. As one newspaper after another retold the tale of Salem Budzyner, Australia's richest and arguably most powerful television program, Channel Nine's '60 Minutes', asked Burstyner for his story.

Burstyner explained to the program's producers that he was building the Baruch case and planned to return to Zurich in January 1997. Within days the '60 Minutes' production team had a deal for Burstyner. They would pay expenses to Switzerland if Burstyner allowed a camera crew to go along for ride. By January Burstyner, Stephen Baruch and Marta Weyland were back in Zurich and this time a top-rating television show was paying the bills. They stayed in the Grand Dolder, one of Zurich's best hotels which had been serving the city since 1899.

In Switzerland the ongoing revelations concerning the position of Swiss banks during the Nazi era had prompted a painful review of the true nature of Swiss neutrality in World War II. The issue was rarely out of the headlines. Arriving in the third week of January the Australian group entered the city as coverage of the affair reached a crescendo. Only days earlier the Christoph Meili story had broken; the 'Meili' affair would do more to propel the issue of Holocaust assets onto the international agenda than any other single event.

Doing his nightly rounds as a security guard in the vaults of Union Bank of Switzerland, Meili entered a basement room in the archives division to find a pile of historic prewar banking documents loaded for a paper shredder. He was stunned at the sight before him. Above, on the streets of Zurich Swiss bankers were telling the nation each day that they had nothing to hide. The president of the very bank where Meili was working had called Holocaust-era funds 'peanuts' only months earlier. So why were the documents being shredded?

Meili would later state the papers were documents relating to the forced sale of properties in Germany. In publicising the shredding activity at UBS, Meili had taken a major risk. As a security guard he had no right to go near bank documents of any era.

Meili took away an armload of documents and decided to alert the Jewish community through Zurich's Israeli Cultural Centre. In doing so he made a decision that would change his life. Meili publicised his find on 14 January, creating a worldwide sensation. For his efforts he was suspended by Union Bank of Switzerland for breaking banking secrecy laws.

As the Swiss press and international agencies took up the story with renewed vigour Burstyner and his plaintiffs accompanied by the '60 Minutes' crew paid a second visit to Swiss Bank Corporation.

In this atmosphere of high tension the meeting with the normally staid SBC officials took on an entirely different tone than Burstyner's previous meeting in 1995.

In his briefcase Burstyner had details of the Budzyner account number and the amounts involved, but the bankers' first tactic was to hold out for more evidence. As the conversation dragged on Burstyner recalled to *The Australian* newspaper how he rose from the table to walk around the room and noticed an old folder jutting out from a pile of papers amassed by one of the bankers. 'I don't know why and I don't know where I got the nerve, but I leant over and took the file out. One look and I knew we had struck on something amazing,' he explained.[4]

Burstyner had grabbed the bank's original file on Budzyner. Inside it he found four bank statements detailing a deposit of 600 pounds sterling made by Budzyner in 1938. The revelation of the original Budzyner documents changed everything. Suddenly the argument no longer turned on whether Stephen Baruch had a case against SBC, the question now was what did SBC owe the Baruch family? Almost immediately Burstyner was in a position to file a formal claim for more than A$800 000 which SBC said it would consider in due course.

Arriving back in Melbourne Burstyner knew he was close to success but the yawning gap between the Bahnhofstrasse and Acland Street, St Kilda quickly threatened to surface again as a stream of faxes poured back and forth between the bank and the offices of Glennen, Burstyner and Company.

Five months would pass and then a deal was struck. As Burstyner explained: 'In the end it was so simple, they just agreed and that was that. I was amazed, I was thrilled. There was so much emotion wrapped up in the case.'[5] Burstyner released details of his success in late July. He knew his life would change forever when he was woken at dawn by a foreign correspondent from the BBC the morning the story appeared in the press.

Early reports said the final settlement was in the order of A$200 000 but Stephen Baruch has since gone on the record saying the payout was actually much smaller than that estimate, though he has never revealed the final figure.

The Baruch story marks the beginning of the heirless assets issue in Australia, and Stephen Baruch has reluctantly taken on the mantle as a battler against the Swiss banks in Australia. He has returned to his work as an accountant with Jewish community services in Sydney, but the case still baffles the 66-year-old Polish gentleman who never sought the limelight. Baruch says, 'People ask me why did the Swiss banks give in to you—I have no idea, they are still a most mysterious group of people if you ask me.'[6]

Chapter three

WHAT DID THEY DO WITH THE MONEY?

What exactly did the Swiss banks do with the money, like the 600 pounds sterling belonging to Salem Budzyner, which was held in the vaults for more than 50 years? They invested wisely and became the richest banks in the world.

The heirless assets which lay in thousands of dormant accounts would become an integral part of the seed capital for powerhouse banks such as Credit Suisse and the newly merged Swiss Bank Corporation and Union Bank of Switzerland—now called United Bank of Switzerland—which is the biggest bank in Europe. Acting as lenders to major corporations and some of the world's richest private clients the Swiss banks could use the funds left in dormant accounts as capital to kickstart new lending programs in the years after the war.

Separately, looted gold from across war-torn Europe, including gold ornaments and even gold teeth from the concentration camps, would mature in the coffers of a string of banks, especially the central bank—the Swiss National Bank. But these dark secrets of the Swiss banking system would remain hidden for decades until the issue of Holocaust assets exploded into the spotlight in 1996.

In the immediate aftermath of World War II, Switzerland's ambiguous neutrality was at its most delicate. It was during this period as a new Europe reasserted itself in the form of the Common Market that Switzerland ran the greatest risk of alienation from European trade flows. It might have been reduced to a regional economy—a minor player in the new Europe's financial system—if not for a sophisticated diplomacy practised by bankers and politicians alike which rekindled the nation's role as a safe harbour for the slush funds of the world.

The suppression of key wartime US intelligence files that clearly showed Switzerland's two-faced role in World War II had assisted in this process. In 1996, however, historians began to reassess Switzerland as hundreds of crucial wartime files were released in Washington under the US Government's 50-year rule for secret reports. Among the most important of these documents were files from the Operation Safe Haven Report which concerned the activities of a special unit within the US Treasury which had been charged with tracking Nazi money in the years after the war. A second crucial set of papers were the 'Red House' documents which detailed Switzerland's proposed role in helping top Nazis escape Europe in 1945.

Reading these documents historians began to recognise that Switzerland as a neutral state was viewed by Germany as being of considerably more use than it might have been as just another captured territory within the Reich. At the very epicentre of Switzerland's compromised neutrality was the banking system. At the state level the Swiss Government through the Swiss National Bank and the Bank for International Settlements (BIS) could receive gold looted by the Nazis in turn for foreign currency to pay for the war effort. Private banks could also provide much needed foreign currency while providing additional services including discreet secret accounts for individual Nazis who were making a fortune out of looting occupied countries.

Switzerland is a small country with very big banks. Zurich may well sit alongside New York or Hong Kong as a financial centre but it certainly does not rank with these metropolitan centres as a city.

Likewise, the nation of Switzerland, despite its high international profile as both a tourist and business centre, is a small state by world standards with a total population of six million. This population is spread quite evenly throughout the country and the administration of the state is highly decentralised.

For the banks the demographics are close to perfection—big banks can push small governments around. In Switzerland the bureaucrats in cantonal governments that make up the nation's public service are no match for the elite corps of highly educated, well-rewarded executives of the 'big two' banks. This is as true today as it was in 1939.

Coupled with power-sapping decentralisation is Switzerland's neutrality which the banks could very well proclaim as an intangible asset. Switzerland more or less defined the historic notion of neutrality during the Thirty Years War in the seventeenth century. The Congress of Vienna in 1815 recognised Switzerland's neutrality and enshrined the alpine state as a buffer zone between Germany and France. Switzerland galvanised its reputation as a non-combatant peacekeeping nation with a long humanitarian tradition embodied in the Red Cross, which was founded in Geneva by Jean-Henri Dunant in 1863. The Geneva Convention, still regarded as the template for behaviour inside war zones, emerged from Geneva a year later in 1864.

By the 1930s the notion of Swiss neutrality was sacrosanct, Switzerland had no intention of entering the war on either side. A plan to defend Switzerland by closing off the railway tunnels and defending the nation from the alps was well publicised but there is evidence the ruling elite of the country never took the plan very seriously.

From the perspective of some Swiss bankers and lawyers, wartime would not be so much 'business as usual' as business that would be too good to be refused. Of course, many Swiss citizens both today and 50 years ago had nothing to do with the machinations of a morally corrupt banking system; they were virtually powerless to stop it providing a service for the Nazis.

In times of war, gold becomes the currency of chaos. During the Second World War the Reichsmark was useless as an item of tradeable currency; as a result foreign currency had to be acquired by the Nazis to pay for the machinery of war. The armaments, the spare parts and the chemicals which were crucial to Germany's plan to dominate Europe could not be bought with Reichsmarks. Instead the Nazis raided and looted every occupied country in Europe to collect gold and other items tradeable as foreign currency. This is documented in the Operation Safe Haven Report released in Washington by the Clinton administration. When the Nazis went to the Swiss banking system with this contraband, the banking authorities—particularly the Swiss National Bank—did not ask any questions.

The Nazis plundered gold from every conceivable source. Once the gold bars from the central banks of occupied countries had been sold, the Nazis took gold from the museums, the streets, and the camps. At the Nuremburg War Trials, Oswald Pohl, the Chief of the Economic Office of the SS, recalled a discussion on looted Jewish valuables with the Vice-President of the Reichsbank, Emil Pohl, which concerned 'rings, watches, eyeglasses, gold bars, wedding rings, brooches, pins, gold fillings and other valuables'.[1]

In a war of unrivalled devastation, where the conventions of battle which had lasted centuries were jettisoned in the face of twentieth-century technology, the Nazis were brutally rapacious. They even set up a looting division—the Devisenschutzkommando DSK—which was made up of SS guards who were authorised to collect gold from anywhere they could find it.

Documents from the Supreme headquarters of the Allied Expeditionary Force (Shaef) from May 1945 show the depths to which Nazis would sink in the search for gold. In the neutered nomenclature of global finance spoken by Swiss bankers to this day, it is called 'non-monetary gold'. In reality, it was gold that was held outside banks—in synagogues, on dining-room tables, or in galleries. It also included dental gold—gold that was pulled from the mouths of Jews, dead or alive, in the concentration camps. The fillings were extracted by fellow prisoners known as Sonderkommandos, who pulled the teeth from the corpses left in the gas chambers.

Meanwhile, the private banks of Switzerland enriched themselves by sitting on the spoils of war—secret accounts flush with funds from Jews and Nazis alike. Among the noted Nazi customers were Anton Burger, an aide to Adolf Eichmann, and Heinrich Hoffman, Hitler's official photographer. Franz Von Papen, the Deputy Chancellor of the Reich, also used the Swiss banking system, putting half a million Swiss francs in the Reifessenkasse Bank. Hitler reportedly had a secret account with Union Bank of Switzerland in Bern where he kept the substantial royalties from *Mein Kampf*, which had been a bestseller inside the Reich, especially after it was pushed on to the school curriculum. US intelligence files indicate that this account was managed for Hitler by Max Amann, one of his key commercial advisers and a highly successful publisher who had the weight of the Nazi party behind him.

For many years it had been assumed that when the Swiss designed the secret accounts in the mid 1930s they were creating a loophole for the Jewish merchants of Europe. But this presumption has now been challenged by the revelation of Nazi names on wartime accounts. The Swiss did not ask questions when people opened secret accounts. The accounts were for money, the depositors did not matter; names were secondary, lodgements were first.

At its simplest, a customer—or more likely a third party such as a Swiss lawyer who was acting for the customer—would arrange to open a secret account. From its inception the account would only be known by its number. The number would be known only to the customer and by one director of the bank who could not disclose the identity of the customer to anybody even other members of the bank.

In the event a third party was used, that middleman also knew the number. If the middleman's client failed to reappear after the war the temptation to withdraw the money in a secret account was great. As claimants would discover when they returned to the banks after the war the elaborate structures which banking secrecy required could cost them dearly. At their worst the structures created opportunities for the unscrupulous while often making it impossible for legitimate claimants to access family funds.

Heavy penalties were introduced for breaking the rules of secrecy surrounding the accounts; rules which exist to this day. In effect the penalties enshrine the system with an aura of state-sanctioned legitimacy. The safeguards created by the Swiss banking system were world class. Many financial administrations in other countries would later try to rival Switzerland as a haven for 'mobile' money. Curacao, the Cook Islands or Jersey would all make a claim on the business, but no administration could compete with Switzerland's state-backed system.

A Swiss bank customer using a secret account for whatever purpose was protected by a watertight legal framework. The Swiss 1934 Law Relating to Banks and Savings Banks says:

> Anyone who in his capacity as an officer or employee of a bank, or as an auditor of his employee, or as a member of the banking commission or an officer or employee of this bureau who intentionally violates his duty to observe silence or his professional rule of secrecy to anyone who induces or attempts to induce a person to commit any such offence, shall be liable to a fine of up to 20 000 francs or imprisonment for up to six months or both.

It was not until the 1970s that Switzerland convinced its banking administration that reforms were needed to the secrecy laws. In 1977 the SBA introduced a new ruling that middlemen or agents opening secret accounts had to have proof they 'knew' who the real owner of the account was and that the funds being deposited were not acquired illegally. This ruling was updated in 1991 when all residual loopholes which allowed agents to get around the 1977 ruling were closed off. As Ulrich Pfister, sitting in his office inside the Bahnhofstrasse offices of Credit Suisse, explains: 'Today it is very clear, a Swiss bank must now know and identify the beneficial owner of any bank account'.[2]

Despite these new rules two things remain the same: the accounts are secret, nobody need know they are there except the account holder; and the banks operate in a neutral country exempt from the majority of the western world's conventional trading obligations.

Few countries have ever held the banking industry in such high regard. But in recent times the image of secrecy which has bolstered the Swiss banking system for decades has been diluted as the more spectacular abuses of the system have been revealed through the courts. These cases have displayed an enduring fashion for Swiss banks among the world's despots and international criminals. Zaire's Mobutu Sese Seko was a particularly loyal client of Swiss banks, and while he was recovering from cancer in the 1970s he was allowed to recuperate in Switzerland to the disgust of international human rights agencies. Haiti's 'Baby Doc' Jean Claude Duvalier, Pakistan's Benazir Bhutto, and the Philippines Ferdinand Marcos have all kept secret accounts in Switzerland.

Marcos, who looted the Philippines to the extent that the country is still in a period of reconstruction more than a decade after his fall from power, kept money in no less than six different Swiss banks. In April 1998 a Zurich judge, Peter Cosandey, who was at the centre of a long-running legal battle over Marcos money in Switzerland, offered a rare glimpse into the levels of wealth washing through the Swiss banking system.

Marcos lodged roughly US$520million with Swiss banks during the period of his regime. In the years following his downfall a legal dispute emerged between the claimants of the money and the Swiss authorities. Making claims on the funds were 10 000 Filipinos who were promised US$2 billion in compensation after the fall of the Marcos regime, the Government of the Philippines, and the Marcos family.

In the preceding months lawyers for the Marcos family had been battling to keep the money safe and secret in Switzerland. Cosandey told a packed courtroom on 21 April 1998 that US$300 million had been transferred to the Philippine National Bank in Manila. The Marcos family then launched a new wave of legal action to retain the rest of the millions in Switzerland.

The dealings of Marcos and other crooked rulers with the banks have come to light in unusual circumstances where the clients have lost control of their assets and the new ruling regime in their home countries has invariably prompted Switzerland into some form of cooperation.

The marketing of Swiss banks is discreet. Couched in double-speak the banks are old hands at selling services which can mean almost anything to anyone. Global asset management is perhaps the phrase that most perfectly reflects the glossy parlance used for hiding rich people's money. In contrast, intermediaries that sell services on the back of Swiss banks, such as US-based financial advisers, do not beat around the bush. They openly promote Swiss banks as safe havens for customers who might not be welcome elsewhere. One recent advertisement from a US financial adviser typifies this approach. The prospective customer is told that civil offences will not cause a Swiss bank to freeze and transfer funds back to a client's country of origin or residence. The reader is additionally comforted by the reminder that only criminal offences under Swiss law will lead to full cooperation with the Swiss authorities. Swiss bank customers are told that a Swiss banker will do absolutely everything to protect a customer's secrecy. Instructions are never carried out in the name of the client but in the code name used for the account. This means the clerk involved in the transaction will not know who is behind the deal. Customers are further protected against 'frivolous lawsuits' by the certainties of the Swiss banking system.

This is the sort of marketing spin on Swiss bank accounts that can be found in the small advertisements in international financial magazines. The idea is to maximise every opportunity to make money and to squirrel it away from prying eyes once it has been collected. For those who wish to conceal their names behind codes and to avoid the irritation of 'frivolous lawsuits' the Swiss banks are there to lend a hand, just as they were 50 years ago.

Jewish customers of Swiss banks in the lead-up to war fell into a wide range of client categories, not all of them honest. Jewish customers were just as likely to use the banks to hide money, to evade tax, or to construct elaborate schemes which in some way arbitraged between the tax systems of the nation states across Europe. But there is a crucial factor which underpinned the fashion for Swiss accounts among Jewish families in the Nazi era—these people were not in a position to trust their own state banking systems.

By the mid 1930s inside Germany, Jews were being forced to hand over their wealth and business enterprises to state authorities for no other reason than the fact they were Jewish. From Denmark to Yugoslavia Jewish families watched the actions of the Nazis inside Germany and hurriedly attempted to make provisions for an uncertain future. They trusted Swiss neutrality as deeply as they trusted the secrecy espoused by Swiss bankers; they were to be bitterly disappointed on both fronts.

With the current furore over dormant accounts the Swiss banks have woken to a publicity nightmare so ferocious it has rubbed off on the image of Switzerland itself. That image of a peace-loving alpine retreat had been carefully cultivated in the postwar period as Switzerland scrambled to capitalise on the new world order after 1945. Carl Jung, a Zurich resident and one of the founding fathers of psychoanalysis, opined in the 1940s: 'the relation of Zurich to the world is not spiritual, it is commercial'.

In the decades after World War II the Swiss Government fostered 'clean' industries such as precision engineering and food processing, while the banking system acquired an image of sophistication and mystique far removed from the reality of its grim trade with the Nazis. As this image reinforced itself Switzerland became one of the world's favourite retreats—the rich and famous clustered around the skiing resorts and lakes. Comedian Charles Chaplin took a house by Lake Geneva, setting a trend which is followed to this day by celebrities including actor Roger Moore and singing star Shirley Bassey. In the 1950s Ian Fleming, the creator of James Bond, would regularly mention Swiss banks in his novels as exotic, fashionable locations in the world of high finance.

By early 1996 'the grilles of the great Swiss banking corporation' would begin to rattle as the relentless stream of wartime revelations hit the press. In its attempts to tame the media the Swiss Bankers Association enlisted top ranking public relations consultants to improve its image. The most powerful of these companies was New York-based Kekst and Company, which the SBA hired to run the worldwide press relations campaign on the dormant accounts issue.

Separately, the Swiss Federal Council retained the public relations services of two New York-based public relations firms—Ruder Finn and Barbour, Griffith and Rogers—to improve the national image of Switzerland. By that time the Swiss really needed professional help in the public relations department because the handling of the Holocaust-era accounts had unmasked an arrogant and insensitive cadre of bankers who were not used to any form of public scrutiny.

Internal estimates from the Swiss banking industry as to the value of dormant accounts relating to the Holocaust-era had always been viewed as suspiciously low considering the scale of banking activity which had occurred prior to the war. Those suspicions were then multiplied by a Swiss Federal councillor, Kasper Villager, when he announced blithely that the argument surrounding dormant accounts was a private affair between Jewish groups and the Swiss banking system.

In May 1996 after a barrage of negative publicity in the international media, Switzerland and its banking community were party to a memorandum of understanding which moved to establish an independent commission chaired by former Swiss Federal Reserve Chairman Paul Volcker to examine the matter of dormant accounts. Shortly after this the Swiss Government also formed its task force responsible for coordinating the government's response to the issue of Holocaust assets. The group was to be led by Special Ambassador Thomas Borer. But the Swiss had left it very late to begin a diplomatic initiative. The world had already been watching for months as Swiss bankers and bureaucrats failed miserably to tackle a deeply important issue with anything like the respect it deserved.

A month before the Volcker Commission was announced US Senator D'Amato had put the issue of Holocaust assets on every front page in North America with his high-profile Senate Banking Commission hearings.

D'Amato is what one of his close associates describes as 'the definitive old style politician, one minute he's bulldozing his way through a debate on technical issues, the next minute he's out in the hall kissing babies'.[3] Certainly D'Amato has whatever it takes to make it in US politics, he has served three terms as a senator and he intends to seek a fourth term. He came to prominence during the 'Whitewater' hearings, which were the first serious domestic test of the Clinton administration before the President's personal life became an even bigger threat.

The 'Whitewater' hearings, which examined the business affairs of the Clintons, were held under the auspices of D'Amato's personal fiefdom, the Senate Banking Committee. Now he was using the same forum to create a high-profile inquisition of the Swiss banking administration.

On 10 June 1996, Senator D'Amato ignited the debate over Swiss neutrality highlighting a secret Holocaust assets deal between Switzerland and Poland signed in 1949. At the heart of this deal was a ruthless anti-Semitism displayed by powerful postwar factions in both Switzerland and communist Poland. The intensity of this anti-Semitism is all the more apparent when set against the period in question—the immediate postwar years were marked by enormous international empathy with Jewish refugees, witnessed most forcefully in the support for the new state of Israel founded in 1948.

In essence the Swiss–Polish deal of 1949 was a bilateral compensation treaty which allowed Poland to pay Switzerland 53 million Swiss francs in compensation for nationalising Swiss assets captured in Poland after the war. In turn the Swiss handed back Polish bank accounts and insurance policies which had lain dormant since the Holocaust. D'Amato's statements on the secret agreement were compounded by new evidence which came to light in Europe that Switzerland had also refused to hand over millions of dollars worth of German assets held in Switzerland to the Allies after the war.

Inside Switzerland the torrent of negative attention from the world press began to have an impact. As the nation's bankers and bureaucrats struggled to present a cohesive response to the flood of accusations, Swiss citizens—particularly Swiss students—began to protest at the inadequacies of the government's response.

By the end of 1996 Switzerland had made a string of compensatory gestures towards the growing lists of claimants, including Gizella Weisshaus who had launched a US$20 billion action against the Swiss banks out of New York.

Among the most important of these moves was the independent expert commission chaired by the noted Swiss historian Jean-Francois Bergier, which would examine Switzerland's role in World War II. While the Volcker Commission would investigate Switzerland's banking system, Bergier would examine the role of the country itself. However, not all Swiss were pleased with the eyes of the world peering relentlessly into their historic dealings with the Nazis.

Just as Studer had typified the arrogance of the banks earlier in the year, Jean Pascal Delamuraz, the President of the Swiss Confederation, found it impossible to contain his sentiments in an interview on 31 December 1996. He told the *Tribune de Geneve* that Switzerland was being exposed 'to attempts at ransoming and blackmail over Holocaust accounts'.

In what was now a recurring nightmare for Switzerland the comments of Delamuraz were picked up by news agencies and run as further evidence of the country's insensitivity to Holocaust survivors.

In the new year, 1997, a Swiss newspaper, *Sonntagszeitung*, reported a leaked confidential report signed by the Swiss Ambassador in Washington, Carlo Jagmetti, who described the Holocaust assets affair as 'a war that must be won'.[4] Within 24 hours Jagmetti was forced to hand in his resignation—Switzerland's ratings on the public relations barometer had reached an all-time low.

But if one incident could be said to have triggered the surge in worldwide activity surrounding the restitution of Holocaust assets it was the story of the Swiss security guard Christoph Meili. When Henry Burstyner and Stephen Baruch had arrived in Zurich in January 1997 the Meili incident had just hit the headlines. The aftermath of this incident and Meili's treatment by Swiss authorities in the following months made the world pay attention to the battle between Jewish claimants and the Swiss administration.

With ham-fisted arrogance UBS had made the situation worse by treating Meili harshly. Meili was arrested and then he was suspended by the bank for breaking Swiss banking laws. In the months following his suspension Meili became both a martyr for the cause of Holocaust assets and a hated figure among a fiercely nationalistic element within Switzerland.

Meili received a string of death threats in the early months of 1997 before he moved to New York where he was granted refugee status. There his case was taken up by Edward Fagan, who was already running a major class action against the banks inside the United States.

With the international media hungry for more detail on the unfolding story of Holocaust assets Meili became a minor celebrity almost overnight. While Union Bank of Switzerland—caught interfering with historical documents at a crucial moment in its relations with Holocaust survivors—took the prize as the most unpopular of the big Swiss banks.

The Swiss then decided to take a new approach in their ongoing confrontation with Jewish groups. By mid 1997 both the Swiss banking system and the Swiss Government were running a series of advertisements and publishing information brochures on the Holocaust assets affair. The advertising copy from both groups used a common theme: the banks would do everything in their power to settle the issue in a fair and equitable manner. But behind the scenes the banks could be as cold and indifferent as ever. The story of Jakov Kaldor, a retired chemist from Melbourne, and his battle with Union Bank of Switzerland reveals in compelling detail the true nature of Swiss banks.

As the Nazi war machine rolled across Europe to the shores of the eastern Mediterranean in 1941, Jakov Kaldor, the son of a Yugoslav businessman, was far removed from the battles being fought in the Balkans. Jakov was in the Swiss Alps at Glarriseg, a boarding school on the shores of Lake Constance. In the tradition of elite Swiss boarding schools still witnessed today at schools such as Le Rosey, the Winterthur-based Glarriseg was a beacon for the world's wealthy and powerful—the Thai royal family traditionally sent their sons to the school.

Like Swiss neutrality itself, the peace of Jakov's lakeside idyll was an illusion. By late 1942 the school had stopped receiving payments from Jakov's parents and suddenly the realities of wartime began to dawn on the schoolboy when his homeland came under Nazi occupation.

Jakov's father, Samuel Kaldor, was a wealthy and assimilated Jew from Dubrovnik, the beautiful walled seaport of Yugoslavia which had included a small Jewish population since the Middle Ages. At the outbreak of World War II in 1939 the Jewish population of Yugoslavia was around 70 000. The Jewish minority in Yugoslavia was not immune to the pogroms and anti-Semitism of Eastern Europe. There are reports of Christian attacks on Jews in the fifteenth and sixteenth century. But in general the area of Dalmatia was a relatively benign environment for Jewish families. Jewish refugees from Spain and Portugal had made Dubrovnik their home over the centuries and the city held about 5000 Jews at the outbreak of the war.

Outside the city walls of wartime Dubrovnik and just a few hours drive up the coast lay a completely different environment—the Ustasi-dominated region of Croatia and its capital of Zagreb. Croatia was ruled by the fiercely anti-Semitic Ante Pavelic. In the puppet Nazi state of independent Croatia more than 20 000 Jews were murdered at the Jasenovac concentration camp while thousands more were deported. The Ustasi regime was ruthless in its hunt for Jewish assets. In Croatia wealthy Jews were arrested almost immediately after the occupation and their families were told to pay 100 kilograms of gold for their release.

In Dubrovnik, however, the Italians were in control and the ruling regime was much less harsh. The Italians generally refused to deport Jews and did not practise anti-Semitism inside their occupied territories. Despite the relative comfort offered by the Italian regime, the outbreak of the war had forced Samuel Kaldor to make major changes to the way he did business.

He had a wide variety of business interests including properties and merchant shipping. In addition he was a partner in a merchant bank, the Dubrovnik-based Exchange Bank. The Kaldor family lived in the Pere Badmani district of the city, where Jakov's sister Magda still lives today.

Fifty years after the war Magda and her sister Cecilia Sejedin, who lives in Mar del Plata, Argentina, found themselves acting together with Jakov in a case against the Union Bank of Switzerland. Now 73, Jakov and his Serbian wife Betty (Borjanka) have been in

Australia for more than 40 years. Their battle with the bank has lasted throughout their adult lives.

At times UBS appeared conciliatory towards the Kaldors, and at other junctures the bank has treated them in a peremptory manner. On at least one occasion it has been obvious the case is being viewed differently by separate divisions within UBS. More than any other Australian case the Kaldors' dealing with UBS displays the alarming gap between the slick public relations presentation the Swiss banks can mount for the media and the heartless bureaucracy which often presides behind closed doors.

In 1939 Samuel Kaldor held an account with Union Bank of Switzerland and invited two business associates to join him as co-signatories. The three men used a common family name Gruen as an alias for the account. Samuel Kaldor was Philippe Gruen, Joseph Mandl was Jakob Gruen and Peter Sutic was Paul Gruen. Assets were deposited in the account in the form of cash, gold and other financial instruments. The value of the account was estimated at 164 000 Swiss francs in January 1964. As Jakov explains:

43

I was in Glarriseg when war came to my home town and I had to finish school early but I was not about to go back to Dubrovnik. The Yugoslav consul in Bern knew me and he looked after my interests for a while. I stayed on in Switzerland basically just letting time pass. The consulate became my home and they gave me some money to survive, it was a strange time for me having directly come out of the protected world of a boarding school.

There must have been almost a year of this strange life in Zurich waiting for the war to end. I am trying to remember how we passed our days, it is difficult to say, we were young you know, there was always people meeting in cafes or whatever, talking about how the war was going, talking about life in general.

Sometime in 1944 a friend and I were pretty sure the war was over at least as far as France was concerned. We had this idea we would leave Switzerland and we made plans to leave and cross the French border. It was really a big adventure for two schoolboys. I remember leaving the city and travelling to the border

area and something went wrong. Pretty soon afterwards
we were captured by Swiss border guards and they put
us in prison because we did not have proper papers. We
ended up in prison for quite a long time,
a few months anyway, and then the war ended and we
were released.

Of course if I had known all the time my family had
money in an account at Union Bank of Switzerland in
Zurich, that would have made a difference. My father
had been in a position to see the deteriorating
situation of Jews in Yugoslavia in the lead-up to the
war. He was a sensible man and he knew when it was
time to make special plans for the future, that is why
he dealt with UBS.

My father died of natural causes in 1940 and his two
partners also died during the war, we know one of them
died in a concentration camp, the other was never
traced. After the war in 1946 I went back to Dubrovnik
and found that my eldest sister Magda had survived the
war in the city, while my other sister Cecilia had
also survived spending most of her time in Yugoslavia.
We were not sure what to do with ourselves but before
I knew what was happening I found myself doing
military service for a year, they had me teaching
geography to soldiers.

After one year's service in the army I met Betty [nee
Vurdlja] who was from Belgrade. Betty and I were going
out together and eventually we got married in Belgrade
in 1948. Once we were married we thought about getting
away from Europe and going to Israel.

Of course at that time the communist government under
Tito was slow to allow most people to leave the
country, but they were happy to allow people like us
to go to Israel if we renounced our citizenship. In
reality that meant renouncing your rights to all
properties in Yugoslavia and handing your inheritance
over to the communist regime.

Anyway we decided to quit Yugoslavia and just get out
there and then. We emigrated to Israel and we stayed
there for nearly seven years. I spent most of my time
working in Akko in local laboratories. Israel was very
tough in those days, there was very little there. I
remember we wanted eggs so we went off and got some
chickens and pretty soon we had eggs all over the place.

But I also remember that the area we were living in was very beautiful. I remember the water being so clear. I would regularly go out fishing with these Arab fisherman and take home my share of what we caught, when I think about this I realise they were very different days.

It was at least six months before I actually managed to get paid some of my salary. But that was the way it went, you bought what you could on credit. Having said that there was very little in the shops, people had to be very self-sufficient.

Though we were working in Israel we were not very settled and we started to think more and more about going to Australia. The main issue at that time was getting someone to sponsor your trip, and we did not have any relatives in Australia or anything like that. But I remember my father had a friend who was a very influential man in England, a Mr Teddy Gardner of the Wembley Rotary Club. He was very involved in the international Rotary Club organisation, and he had a good relationship with our family from the time he had come to Dubrovnik to establish the Rotary Club in Yugoslavia.

I wrote to Mr Gardner in London and told him our case and of our desire to emigrate to Australia. Through his offices we were lucky enough to have our passage arranged. We were able to get the Rotary Club of Essendon to sponsor us. The Rotary Club did terrific work for us. When we came out they had a welcoming committee to meet us off the ship at Port Melbourne. They also arranged that we had a house in Moonee Ponds where we were able to stay for the first few weeks when we arrived. It was 1956, the year of the Olympics, it was a nice time to arrive in Australia.

Shortly after their arrival in Melbourne Jakov Kaldor began what has evolved into a marathon battle with Union Bank of Switzerland. Working with his sisters in Yugoslavia and Argentina, the family has kept a remarkable record of their case with the bank by preserving the majority of letters sent between the two parties. The correspondence began in 1948 when the Kaldors first asked UBS about their case. The letters have mostly been written in German by UBS and translated into English by the Kaldors.

Jakov Kaldor also retains a fascinating letter from February 1957 when the debate with UBS seemed close to a resolution. In the course of the letter the bank confirmed that Jakov's father Samuel Kaldor, using the name Philippe Gruen, had an account at the bank, which contained an unquantified amount of money. The bank demanded death certificates of all three business associates from Dubrovnik, even though it was clear that at least one of the partners had died in a concentration camp.

Despite the difficulties put forward by the bank, the letter indicated the possibility of restitution to the Kaldors. But initial attempts by the family to make progress with the bank were marred by the complications of running a case against the bank from three different countries. The Kaldors wrote to the bank regularly—the family still have letters from October 1957 and October 1962—but real progress continued to elude them.

Like thousands of other families dealing with the banks the Kaldors got on with their lives in the decades after the war and they let the case remain dormant. It was only in 1997 with the worldwide resurgence of pressure against the banks that the family decided to revive the case.

Two letters sent between 15 May and 22 May 1997 show UBS giving completely different advice to the family. What is more, the letters both arrived at the Kaldors' family home in Melbourne on the same day. The most telling aspect of the correspondence is the curt tone of a letter written on 16 September 1997 when the bank responded to news the family has appointed a solicitor after more than 50 years of dealing with the bank privately through official channels. The three-paragraph letter deals with the family as if they were unknown to the bank; the contrast with the helpful tone of full-page advertisements sponsored by UBS at the time in Australian newspapers could not be more dramatic.

Union Bank of Switzerland

Mr Jakov Kaldor
Doncaster
Melbourne Zurich
16 September 1997

Annne-Hoz/tel 01/234 4724
Estate of the late Mr Samuel Kaldor (alias Philippe Gruen)

Dear Mr Kaldor

We refer to the previous correspondence with you and Mrs Cecilia Segedin-Kaldor and have to advise you than an account with above mentioned deceased has not been in existence for the last ten years with our head office in Zurich.

Owing to the prevailing legal stipulations in Switzerland we have to preserve files for the term of ten years. Therefore the account mentioned in the correspondence sent to us by Mrs Segedin-Kaldor must have been closed before 1987.

We are sorry that we are not in a position to give you a more satisfactory answer. We kindly ask you to inform Mrs Segedin-Kaldor about this letter.

Yours sincerely,

Union Bank of Switzerland

Signed off by two assistant vice-presidents, the letter reveals nothing of the four-decade history behind the affair between the Kaldors and UBS. But the letter gives a rare glimpse into the dead hand of bureaucracy inside the Swiss banks which eroded the confidence of thousands of claimants over recent decades. It was written less than nine months after Christoph Meili had blown the whistle on UBS document shredding and ensured the Zurich bank was public enemy number one for Jewish groups around the world.

The abbreviated content and formal tone of the letter reveals all the problems associated with Switzerland and its banking system; problems which even the world's smartest public relations companies found beyond their capacity to resolve.

Following the dismissive note of 16 September the Kaldors realised there was little hope in continuing to deal with the bank in the manner which had been used over previous years. It was clearly time for advocacy. The solicitor hired by the family was Henry Burstyner, the Melbourne lawyer who had hit the headlines with the Baruch case earlier that year. After hiring Burstyner in September 1997, Jakov Kaldor commented: 'Sometimes, I sit back and I think that despite all their antics the Swiss banks are doing absolutely nothing at all about people like me.'[5]

Jakov Kaldor has retired from his job at the Fairfield Hospital in Melbourne where he worked as a medical researcher. He now watches the press and television every day for any news on the Swiss banks affair. His sister Magda is ill, she is 79 and living in Dubrovnik, while Cecilia is 83 years old and continues to live in Mar del Plata, the coastal city outside Buenos Aires.

In May 1998 Henry Burstyner visited UBS in Zurich after the bank had finally given ground and revealed that as long ago as 1964 it had been established that there were 169 000 Swiss francs in the account used by Samuel Kaldor. Burstyner reached a settlement with the bank that was received with great relief by all sections of the Kaldor family in Buenos Aires, Dubrovnik and Melbourne. While he describes the atmosphere of the negotiations as 'considerably more cordial than ever before' the fact that his discussions with the bank lasted almost four days indicates the negotiations were every bit as arduous as the Baruch case two years earlier.

Burstyner is bound by a confidentiality agreement with UBS and would not reveal any details of the settlement. However, it is understood from sources within the legal community that the settlement is believed to have exceeded A$300 000.

If the Kaldors' story tells us anything about the process of restitution when left to the banks themselves, it is that the process is deeply flawed. Until late 1996 there was no process outside the confines of the banking system. Thousands of Jewish claimants seeking Holocaust funds simply tunnelled away against the enervating bureaucracy revealed in the UBS correspondence with the Kaldor family.

It was only after the crescendo of negative publicity which surrounded the Christoph Meili affair at UBS and the shock resignation of Ambassador Carlo Jagmetti that the Swiss Bankers Association knew it had to act. The time had come to show the world the Swiss banks were not cold-hearted villains.

Working quickly, the Swiss banks decided to make a gesture of compensation. The President of Credit Suisse, Rainer Gut, broke the ice in January 1997 with a suggestion for a humanitarian fund, and the idea was taken up by the Swiss Bankers Association. On 5 February a joint announcement by Credit Suisse, Swiss Bank Corporation and Union Bank of Switzerland said that a humanitarian fund of 100 million Swiss francs would be distributed to victims of the Holocaust.

The announcement signalled a change of heart within Switzerland, but it did little for the thousands of Holocaust survivors claiming individual accounts. The money remained inside the banks, nobody knew how much was there, nobody had any way of checking what the banks had kept since the war.

In March the Swiss Government made its formal response when Arnold Koller, the President of the Swiss Confederation, proposed a major government fund to right the wrongs of the war. To be called the Solidarity Fund and financed by a re-evaluation of the gold reserves inside the Swiss National Bank, half of the proposed 7 billion Swiss francs would be spent inside Switzerland. The rest would be given to foreign victims of human rights violations.

Both funds were welcomed as signals of a new atmosphere within Switzerland. At 7 billion francs the government fund was particularly generous and received a positive response from foreign governments.

In defending their position over heirless assets Swiss bankers constantly sought to spread the issue of blame across the European financial system. 'Why pick on us, there were others', was the refrain from the boardrooms of Zurich. In time a host of European financial institutions would be drawn into the fray, but for the moment it was the nation of Switzerland which reluctantly remained in the spotlight.

As lobbyists, journalists, politicians and academics tried to come to terms with the huge scale of the Holocaust assets issue, attention was focused on the role of Switzerland and the Allies in the period immediately after the war. Analysts began to review the much-maligned Washington Agreement between Switzerland and the Allies of 1946 which was meant to settle the issue of Holocaust assets for all time.

The Washington Agreement had been signed under extraordinary circumstances as the Allies were attempting to rebuild Europe. In 1946 Switzerland was growing in its role as lender to the world. It had thrived during the war and by the time of the agreement negotiations it had enormous leverage in international financial circles.

In contrast, the finances of the Allies were in tatters. Britain was badly in need of Swiss funds. Moreover, Britain still had interests in the

Middle East through the state of Palestine, lobbying for Jewish interests was a delicate issue in 1946. France too was concentrating primarily on rebuilding France, and it knew the country would be needing capital from its newly enriched alpine neighbour in the coming years.

The two most powerful nations at the negotiations were the United States, represented by a tax expert, Randolph Paul, and Switzerland, represented by the bureaucrat Walter Stucki. Inside the negotiating rooms in Washington, the Swiss team argued Switzerland had been weakened during the war and the value of German assets inside its banks was negligible. The Allies argued Switzerland had taken in vast amounts of gold, cash and other valuables during the war and it was time to hand them over to the Allies for repatriation to the rightful heirs.

During the negotiations Stucki vehemently denied Switzerland had knowingly accepted any Nazi gold. At the same time Randolph Paul had Allied intelligence documents which showed Switzerland had taken in at least US$200 million of gold looted by the Nazis.

In retrospect, the Allies should have had the upper hand in these negotiations despite any fears from Britain and France that upsetting the Swiss might bear a cost in the longer term. But the weakness of the Allied negotiators was a lack of agreement on what should be achieved by the accord. The Swiss proved very skilled negotiators; they realised the unity of the Allies was collapsing now that the war was over. Moreover, they knew that, ultimately, the Allies could only achieve restitution by agreement. In the end Switzerland was a sovereign state and the spoils of war remained safe behind its neutral borders.

Classified papers released years after the agreement show the United States was desperate for an agreement. As the Cold War loomed over Europe the fate of Jewish family fortunes trapped inside Swiss banks was not a top priority. As the negotiations continued Switzerland's position grew stronger and stronger. The unity of the Allies was cracking by the day, the pressure being brought to bear by the United States looked like typical US foreign policy bully boy tactics. The longer the talks dragged on the less likely a solid agreement would be signed.

After three months of discussions an agreement was finally signed on 25 May 1946. The agreement, which included Switzerland sharing half of the German wartime assets still held in Swiss banks, included a provision that Switzerland had to pay out US$58 million—less than one fifth of the minimum amount estimated to be in Switzerland's possession in looted gold alone. Negotiations over all other wartime assets acquired by the Swiss were left unresolved. The Swiss promised the Allies that claims, heirless assets such as dormant accounts, insurance policies, art and other valuables would be considered as ancillary to the agreement.

By 1947 it was clear to Jewish groups around the world that the Washington Agreement was a complete failure. The omission by the Allies of any process for the payment of the promised funds or any procedures for the restitution of Holocaust assets meant the agreement virtually lapsed as the Cold War began to dominate Allied policy.

In mid 1948 Walter Stucki visited Washington and explained to US Treasury representatives the various obstacles that had arisen in Switzerland which prevented the country honouring its obligations under the agreement signed three years earlier. At the end of 1948 the failure of the Washington Agreement was plain for all to see.

Seymour Rubin, the US Treasury official responsible for Operation Safe Haven, exclaimed in December 1948 that the Swiss obstinacy on Holocaust assets was 'a thorough perversion of the terms and the intent of the Washington Accord'.[6] In the years after the agreement, Switzerland built an image of cosy neutrality and the bankers locked the doors on their Nazi gold. The country became an ally of the United States in the Cold War, further diluting the impact of the Washington Agreement.

Fortunately for Jewish claimants across the globe today, the US Treasury officials who worked on Operation Safe Haven kept records of their largely fruitless attempts to make the Swiss honour their responsibilities under the Washington Agreement. While they may not have been successful in the late 1940s the files they kept have allowed the hunt for Holocaust assets to resume in the 1990s with a new vigour.

Chapter four

AUSTRALIA
TUNES IN

As Switzerland struggled to contain the growing clamour surrounding the fate of Holocaust assets almost every country in the western world began a revision of its wartime history.

In the United States Senator D'Amato led a broad spectrum of politicians and activists keen to see the issue receive top priority, while in Britain Greville Janner, the high-profile MP for Leicester, loudly demanded a renegotiation of the Washington Agreement. Also in Britain the Foreign Office issued its first report on Nazi gold and early moves were made to sponsor a major international conference on the issue.

In France the issue had exposed a whole new dimension of the anti-Semitism within the wartime Vichy regime. France was the most looted country in Western Europe—one third of all art in private hands was removed by the Nazis during the occupation. In April 1997 a major exhibition of 900 looted art works was staged in Paris by the government in an attempt to locate the rightful owners. Separately, the Chirac administration launched a commission to trace property stolen from French Jews.

The Belgian Central Bank began an investigation into gold transactions with wartime Germany as did the Central Bank of Portugal and the Central Bank of Sweden. The Government of Holland announced that the Van Kemenade Commission would be established to resolve claims relating to the Holocaust era. In Norway a commission was investigating properties confiscated during the Nazi puppet regime led by Vikund Quisling.

In South America both Brazil and Argentina began to study their wartime record. South America had been a major escape route for Nazis after the war ended. Operation Odessa had been launched in the last months of the Reich to ferry key Nazis, including Joseph Mengele—the 'White Angel' of the death camps—to the safety of seclusion in Brazil.

In November 1997 a legal search in Sao Paulo hit the headlines when the court-ordered opening of two safety deposit boxes belonging to a former German immigrant, Albert Blume, revealed 230 gold items including gold bars from the Holocaust era. The find was a major breakthrough for Brazil's Commission for the Search of Nazi Monies. This commission is still investigating more than fourteen wartime-era German accounts which are thought to contain more than US$70 million.

In Australia, with the exception of the Baruch case the affair remained subdued in 1997. The Jewish community had always played a key role in the multicultural mix of Australia; there had been Jews on the First Fleet in 1788. Jews in Australia were a homogenous minority for most of the early nineteenth and early twentieth centuries. The vast majority of Jewish families had emigrated from the United Kingdom, particularly East London.

However, the Second World War would alter that social profile dramatically. In the three decades to 1963 Australia took in around 40 000 Jews who were survivors of the Holocaust. This figure is higher than the total number of Jews who had lived in Australia before the war.

Today with about 10 000 Holocaust survivors still living in Australia, the country has the highest number of Holocaust survivors per capita in the world, excluding Israel. Considering these demographics it was obvious the issue of Holocaust assets would eventually surface on the national agenda as the large Jewish communities of Australia were stirred into action.

Australia's treatment of its Jewish minority has a complex history which has often belied the image of a benevolent host nation that offered a refuge in the darkest days of the Nazi era. While the country took in a relatively large number of Jewish refugees on a per capita basis, studies by academics including Paul Bartrop[1] have shown there had been fierce resistance to Jews as a race from powerful sections of Australia's 'whites only' society at the time. Newspaper coverage from the era shows politicians loudly bemoaning the fact Australia could not attract the Aryan races of Scandinavia and regretting the arrival of Eastern European Jews who were seen to be less acceptable than the assimilated Jews of Great Britain.

In reality Australia did little more than the minimum a free democracy might have been expected to do at the time of World War II. As the issue of Jewish refugees became urgent in the aftermath of Kristallnacht on 9 November 1938, the government of Joseph Lyons and his Interior Minister John McEwen had placed a blanket restriction on the number of refugees allowed into Australia per annum. The Australian policy of allowing a set annual quota of 15 000 refugees into the country had halted what would have been a considerably larger flow of Jewish immigrants in the coming years. This policy of minimalist response had been set in train at the Evian Conference in July 1938 where US President Franklin D Roosevelt had called an international meeting to discuss the looming problem of refugees from the Third Reich.

Speaking at the conference Australia's chief negotiator, Lieutenant Colonel Thomas White, had made it clear to the world that his country had no intention of becoming a safe harbour for all persecuted Jews. In a speech which offered plenty of sympathy but precious little practical support, White said: 'Under the circumstances, Australia cannot do more ... undue privileges cannot be given to one particular class of non-British subject without injustice to others. It will no doubt be appreciated also that, as we have no real racial problems, we are not desirous of importing one by encouraging any scheme of large-scale foreign migration.'[2]

By the time war was in full progress and the stream of immigration requests had turned into a flood, Australia's immigration officials would be able to reassure the press and politicians alike that the country was not extending its resources by taking in more immigrants than had been envisaged in a long-term plan.

Nevertheless, despite the resistance within the bureaucracy to Jewish immigration, Australian-based Jewish pressure groups were instrumental in exploiting every loophole in the Australian immigration policy. Many Jewish families were brought in under 'special circumstances' over and above the official quota set by the government.

After the war Jewish immigration to Australia formed patterns that still exist. In terms of distribution, 'new' Jewish immigrants from Poland, Hungary, Czechoslovakia, Romania, Yugoslavia, Russia, and Germany settled sometimes uneasily with the more assimilated prewar Jews who had mostly arrived from Britain. In the 1950s Melbourne became the city of choice for Polish Jews while Sydney proved more attractive to Hungarian Jews.

As Bill Rubinstein explains in *The Jews in Australia*:

In 1933 Australia's meagre 25 000-strong Jewry was merely the forty-first largest in the world, exceeded by the Jewish populations of virtually every European country as well as that of many Middle Eastern and

Asian nations. Through the catastrophe of the Holocaust and, soon after, widespread migration to the newly founded state of Israel, by 1991 Australian Jewry had become the tenth largest in the world, exceeded only by the Jewish populations of the United States, Israel, USSR, France, Britain, Canada, Argentina, Brazil, and South Africa.[3]

As an ethnic minority Jews have a reputation inside Australia of being highly organised. The truth is a little different; as a minority they have a myriad of organisations but the overall structure of these related groups is often confusing. Several pressure groups overlap and there is no clear pyramidal structure of community power. In contrast to the United Kingdom for example, there is no 'chief rabbi' who acts as a spokesman for the entire community.

This diffuse nature of the minority in Australian society can lead to a dissipation of community initiatives. In marked contrast to the United States where the Jewish minority has traditionally exercised considerable influence on the major centres of power, Jewish groups in Australia are often at the margin of policy-making.

This lack of a national coordinating mechanism for Jewish interests became evident as the Holocaust assets affair unfolded. In effect the Jewish minority often unwittingly kept the issue to themselves. To seasoned observers of Jewish life in Australia this disjointed response to the debate over heirless assets would have come as no surprise. Bill Rubenstein suggested in 1991:

Much that we have discerned as characteristic of the postwar [Jewish] community plainly has at least a part of its source in the number of proportions of Holocaust survivors in Australia, especially in Melbourne: its inwardness, its non-universality, its penchant for establishing separate Jewish institutions, the phenomenal drive to succeed demonstrated by so many migrants, the absolute support given to Israel and the deep disquiet caused by press and media criticism of Israeli actions, no matter how well taken. Melbourne with its large population of Polish Jews who have borne the brunt of the catastrophe far more totally than others, has notably exhibited these characteristics to a greater extent than Sydney whose relatively numerous Hungarians and Germans suffered the massacres (as opposed to the expulsions) less comprehensively than did Polish Jewry, and which had a large pre-existing Anglo-Jewish population.[4]

To many Australian Holocaust survivors the debate surrounding Holocaust assets belittled the separateness of the Holocaust itself. Social workers in the Jewish community moved to protect many Holocaust survivors from further intrusion into their personal history. At its most extreme this drive to protect survivors from intrusion from a younger generation of Australians who cannot hope to fully understand the ramifications of the Holocaust has led occasionally to self-defeating moves by community leaders. As a subject the Holocaust is surrounded with immeasurable difficulty for the survivors and historians alike. These difficulties come to the fore in any project where 'outsiders' attempt to chronicle the Holocaust in any manner.

The dilemmas thrown up by the 'inwardness and non-universality' of Australia's Holocaust survivors were clearly revealed in events surrounding the movie *Schindler's List*. Steven Spielberg's Oscar winning film was based on the original novel *Schindler's Ark* by Australian novelist Thomas Keneally.

Twenty Melbourne-based Holocaust survivors had been among more than 1200 Jews who were saved from almost certain death in the gas chambers when Oskar Schindler put them on his 'list' to work in his ceramic factories. Keneally's novel and later Spielberg's movie would awaken a whole new generation to the lessons of the Holocaust.

Yet both the book and the movie prompted very different reactions from Holocaust survivors including those who were actually saved by Schindler. Joseph Gross, an 89-year-old Melbourne-based survivor declined to be interviewed by Keneally when he was researching the book. Gross lost his first wife, their son, his two sisters, five brothers and their families in the Holocaust. On the release of *Schindler's List*, Gross was finally persuaded to talk about his experience. Asked by Deborah Stone of *The Age* newspaper in Melbourne to comment on Schindler, Gross replied: 'I don't want to praise one German because I survived when all my family perished.'[5]

Following the remarkable success of *Schindler's List* Spielberg launched the Shoah Visual History Foundation. This US$100 million project aimed to create a multimedia history of the Holocaust based on the recorded testimony of Holocaust survivors. In Australia alone the scale of the project required more than one hundred interviewers to record the stories of Australia's dwindling population of survivors, the majority over 60 years of age.

Melbourne quickly became one of the key offices for the foundation in Australia and the project office at Port Melbourne recorded some of the most moving testimonies in the entire project. However, the 'non-universality' of the survivor community surfaced again. In the early stages of the Spielberg project researchers combed the Holocaust survivor groups for interview subjects. The fundamental aim of the project is inclusion, the scale of the project literally allows everyone who survived the Holocaust to take part. But as one researcher explained: 'in some groups, especially among the Holocaust survivor organisations we came upon real resistance, there was a strong sense that the Holocaust belonged to them and they did not want anyone else to get involved'.[6]

To a degree, sections of the Jewish community appeared keen to keep the issue of Holocaust assets to themselves. This inwardness was reflected in the low-profile approach adopted by the Jewish community and the Jewish media. The *Australian Jewish News*, for example, gave far greater coverage to rival issues affecting the national community such as the fallout from the Maccabiah Games tragedy than to the fate of 1000 families who had tried to seek restitution from Swiss banks. In the immediate aftermath of the Christoph Meili affair the mainstream newspapers and television networks ran dozens of stories on 'the lost millions of Australia's Jews'. But in late 1997 the issue would retract again behind the perimeters of the Jewish community.

Why did this occur? There are various answers. The urge to keep Holocaust issues 'inside' the Jewish community contributed to some degree, but a desire to dampen anti-Semitism is probably the major factor.

Pauline Hanson, the radical Queensland politician who led an outwardly racist anti-immigration campaign, was enjoying her first wave of public attention in mid 1997. While a handful of Jewish activists were canvassing support for claimants in the media, many Jewish leaders felt uncomfortable with the coverage of the Holocaust assets affair at a time when Hanson's One Nation Party was gathering strength. A stereotype of rich Jews with secret fortunes stashed away in exotic locations was being revived at a time when racism was on the rise across Australia. Powerful segments of the Jewish community believed the best way to handle the affair was to get it off the front pages and to begin lobbying more discreetly with the Swiss Government and with the banks themselves.

At the same time in Zurich and Basel, the Swiss Bankers Association was preparing an international strategy to deal with the expected deluge of claims from around the world. Despite divisions within Australia's Jewish community, Australia was about to become an integral part of the SBA strategy when senior executives of Switzerland's biggest banks identified four cities as top priority for claimant activity: Tel Aviv, New York, Budapest and Sydney.

Tapping into the restitution structures that had already been formed by the Volcker Commission, the SBA said it would publish a list of dormant accounts. It was a dramatic decision and a major breakthrough for Jewish claimants. The publication of any names relating to dormant accounts could only help Jewish families seeking restitution. Moreover, the exercise was a remarkable move by a banking system which had thrived for generations on its fabled secrecy.

On 25 June Volcker broke the news to the world media. 'This is quite unprecedented in terms of normal banking practice,' said the former Chairman of the US Federal Reserve, a position which is widely regarded as the second most powerful appointment in the American administration after the Presidency.[7]

'You will see the walls of Swiss bank secrecy come tumbling down,' responded the triumphant WJC Chairman Edgar Bronfman.[8]

The effect of the announcement was that while Switzerland's mysterious banking system was not quite laid bare, the gloss was gone, and under the surface were the grubby details of how a major banking system had hidden money from a generation of account holders.

Worse still for the banks, instead of appeasing the demands from at home and abroad for greater transparency, the publication of the first list of 2000 names on 24 July 1997 only whetted the appetite of claimants and observers alike for more information on the role of Swiss banks during and after the war. As the list drew commentary and speculation from every conceivable source, thousands of Jewish families tuned into the affair for the first time. When dozens of Swiss-based names—even residents of Zurich—

appeared on the list it became obvious the SBA could easily have tracked down many of the listed dormant account holders.

Instead of serving as an act of contrition for the Swiss, the list was regarded as an inventory of Swiss guilt. The Swiss banking industry was again caught off its guard and before it could react the affair had escalated to a new level.

In Australia the list was published in *The Australian*, *The Age* and *The Sydney Morning Herald* and created a sensation as the local media scrambled to find anyone connected with the four Australian-based names on the list. At that early stage in the process most Australian commentators did not realise the locations assigned to customers on the list had little relevance in the late 1990s since the list detailed the last known whereabouts of a customer in 1945.

In Australia as in every other jurisdiction the publication of the list prompted a range of reactions. Jewish families reviewed the economic history of their own lives. In the decades since the war, the Swiss banks had taken on a mythical status for many Jewish refugees. Everyone knew someone who might have lived a very different life if they had managed to reclaim what was meant to be deposited in the vaults of Switzerland. Separately, social analysts debated the rights and wrongs of revisiting the past, and financial executives winced at the thought of a resurgence in claimant activity.

While the Jewish community was coming to terms with the new rules for restitution, the SBA's appointment of Ernst and Young as the managers of the claims process came into play. The SBA gave the accountancy group a clear mandate to handle all inquiries and claims against the Swiss banks in relation to dormant accounts. Ernst and Young was to use its worldwide network to receive, filter and process all claims. It could also provide assistance wherever necessary, but ultimately the process ended with the SBA. Final decisions on the merits of any application would be taken in Basel.

In advertisements for the lists which were carried by major newspapers throughout the world, the SBA said the list publication was 'part of a newly created, expedited claims process ... this initiative will be administered by an international board of trustees and supervised by the Swiss Federal Banking Commission and the

Independent Committee of Eminent Persons, chaired by Paul Volcker, that was established to identify dormant accounts of Holocaust victims'.

In Sydney, a Canadian-born Ernst and Young executive John Gibson was given responsibility for the claims process in Australia. Within days of the list publication in Australia, the Sydney office began to receive a stream of potential claims which flowed in consistently over the next six months. Claims were received from every corner of Australia with Melbourne emerging as the largest centre of activity. To their surprise Gibson's team also began to receive inquiries from around the Pacific rim, particularly from Brazil and Argentina.

South America had also been a major refugee centre for Jewish emigrants during the war. In common with Australia, South America had regularly emerged as an alternative for Jews who could not acquire papers to North America. Despite the intense activity surrounding Holocaust assets in both Brazil and Argentina, the SBA had ignored South America when planning its network of Ernst and Young offices. As a result the team in Sydney found they were on the phone to South American Jews on a regular basis.

By the end of 1997 the Australian team had handled more than one thousand inquiries. As these inquiries entered the SBA process the fall-off rate between initial inquiry and formalisation of claims was dramatic. Many claimants had little detail of their family history. Names were missing, dates were missing, most importantly bank names were missing, while account numbers were very rare indeed.

For every five applications that went through the Sydney office only one would be acknowledged by the SBA as a formal claim. The fall-off rate would dash hopes for thousands of Australian Jews but it would rekindle hope for those whose application was accepted.

By 10 December 1997 Ernst and Young was able to publish its first estimate of the formally recognised Australian claims—91 from Victoria, 81 from New South Wales, nine from the Australian Capital Territory, eight each from Queensland and South Australia, five each from Western Australia and New Zealand, and one from Tasmania, representing a total from Australia of 208.

Separately, Ernst and Young in Australia were appointed to handle eleven offshore claims, eight from Argentina, two from the United

Kingdom and one from Brazil. Outside the office of John Gibson the manila folders were lined along the corridor in bundles marked by their language of application. In the following months they would be dispatched to take their place in the towers of applications from around the globe that lined the walls of the Swiss Bankers Association in Basel.

As the dormant accounts process trundled into action it was evident that the dormant accounts would be primarily a Jewish issue and the resolution of the affair would be driven by the international Jewish community. However, the embarrassing presence of Hitler's photographer and other top Nazis on the list reminded the wider public that in Switzerland at least the issue was about 'dormant accounts' not 'Jewish accounts'.

Jewish families had a monopoly on the issue not because they were the only people who used the accounts but because the Swiss had isolated Jewish accounts and refused to hand the money back.

Jewish pressure groups found fault with the Volcker Commission dormant accounts process almost immediately. The core of the problem was that despite the elaborate preparations made for dealing with the banks through the commission, the entire enterprise still revolved around the notion of cooperation. The investigators could not demand documents from the banks which might be crucial to the outcome of any examination of a particular account.

More importantly, the process left loopholes. It dealt with dormant accounts which the bank had control of in the current era. Accounts that were closed or transferred to units within the Swiss Government slipped through the structure created for the Volcker Commission.

While the commission had coverage of dormant accounts opened by individuals, the vast area of accounts opened by family businesses was not comprehensively covered by the agreement. Since so many Jewish merchants worked within the confines of a family business this exclusion was bound to create problems in the future. But at the time the complaints from Jewish pressure groups were ignored. At their worst, the complaints seemed petty and vindictive. After all, the Swiss banks were finally doing their best and working with a major international commission, weren't they?

The experiences of Australian-based claimants such as the Kaldors and the Baruch family have shown that trusting the Swiss 'to do their best' had not been a reliable strategy.

As the publicity surrounding the Swiss bank accounts reached a crescendo it seemed as if Jews and Nazis were the only ones to have left money in Switzerland that the banks did not return. But there were clients from the war era who were neither Jewish nor Nazi—they simply had money in Switzerland and suddenly found themselves in the middle of a maelstrom. One such account holder was Jim Stratmann, a non-Jewish architect from Adelaide who found his name on the front pages of the Australian newspapers after his grandfather, Carl Stratmann, appeared on the first list of dormant accounts.

Carl Stratmann was a confectioner from the town of Krefeld in the Rhineland district of central Germany who emigrated to Australia in 1890. He worked first as a chocolate maker with the McRobertsons confectionery company in Melbourne where he introduced European techniques to Australia. Around the turn of the century, Carl Stratmann moved to Adelaide where he founded his own chocolate company which was an immediate success.

By 1912 Stratmann was very much the prosperous emigrant businessman and he capped his success that year with a return visit to Europe—a rare and very expensive indulgence for Australian immigrants at that time. The Stratmann family made their holiday base in Lucerne, Switzerland, where they stayed on and off for about three months. It was during this time that Carl Stratmann almost certainly opened his Swiss bank account, according to Jim Stratmann.

It is most likely that Carl Stratmann left Lucerne in 1912 without closing this account. Certainly, by the time he returned to Adelaide he had other things on his mind; anti-German sentiment was beginning to be felt across Australia as Kaiser Wilhelm built up Germany's military capacity and relations between Germany and the United Kingdom deteriorated.

On the outbreak of the war in 1914 Stratmann's chocolate business was virtually boycotted by South Australian shoppers, and within months the company was facing a cash-flow crisis. By 1915 Carl Stratmann was beginning to panic when he encountered a wily local entrepreneur, Alfred Haigh.

Haigh was a confectioner who had built a string of successful ice-cream shops around Mount Gambier in South Australia and was looking for a new business in Adelaide. Knowing a bargain when he saw one, Alfred Haigh bought the Stratmann factory and created Haighs chocolates, one of the best known chocolate companies in Australia.

Currently run by Alister Haigh, Alfred's great-grandson, Haighs Chocolates is still headquartered in Adelaide and its chocolates are still made from recipes inherited from Carl Stratmann.

Today Jim Stratmann finds himself in a minority within a minority as a non-Jewish claimant against the Swiss Banks. He says he does not feel isolated amid the Jewish activism which dominates the dormant accounts affair, instead Stratmann says he is mainly curious about the deposit made by his grandfather almost 90 years ago.

'There were other Carl Stratmanns in my family but we are all pretty certain the deposit was made by my grandfather in Lucerne. When I saw my name on the list, it was like a bolt from the blue because it said "C Stratmann—Adelaide" and we could not remember any dealings between my grandfather and Swiss banks until someone mentioned the holiday in 1912.

'For us this is just a curiosity, but I feel sympathy for Jewish families who have been duped over generations by these banks. We've been through all the formalities now and the SBA have acknowledged receipt of our claim, it should be very interesting to see what happens next.'[9]

The publication of the list has allowed some claimants to strengthen their case against the banks. Those who are lucky enough to find their names on it—and they are only a minority of claimants—now have a fighting chance to claim their money. The wider impact of the list's publication, however, was to ignite the entire issue of Holocaust assets for the first time since the war.

By offering a glimpse into the inner workings of the Swiss banking system the SBA list proved that Holocaust assets were a reality. Funds originally deposited by Jewish families from all over the world were held in dormant accounts by Swiss banks for more than 50 years. These families were killed in concentration camps, or died in starvation, or they lived in obscurity behind the Iron Curtain for decades. Alternatively, they fled to the new world. Whatever their story, they were dealt a raw deal by a rich and morally decadent banking system.

The publication of the list by the Swiss Bankers Association represented a watermark in the history of Holocaust asset restitution. At the very least it unveiled a more lenient process for restitution from a banking system which had been cold-hearted, arrogant and anti-Semitic at points in its history.

It made people question for the first time, what happened to my family home? what happened to my father's insurance policy, my uncle's factory … what happened to my mother's diamonds?

Questions were being asked for the first time in a generation; in the coming months answers would be given.

Chapter five

THE SWISS WERE NOT ALONE

Anyone today who is wealthy enough to have a secret Swiss bank account will almost certainly own a range of other valuable assets. Maybe the account holder will have a sizeable life insurance policy, or several bank accounts holding a significant volume of privately held assets. They will almost certainly have a substantial family home, perhaps a holiday home. If they are in business there will be financial assets and the line between personal and corporate wealth may be difficult to define. These investors will not think twice about the security offered by the financial institutions they deal with—they will rely on the brand names which have stood out within the economy over generations. In Australia more than one million families have life insurance policies from either AMP or National Mutual. These families believe they have little reason to fear for the prudential stability and financial integrity of these companies which have stood the test of time. Families in the United States feel the same way about Fidelity, Kemper or Merrill Lynch.

Jewish merchants, mill owners, furriers or doctors in the 1930s were the same in their attitudes as the proud home owners and

shareholders who dot Australia and the United States today. They implicitly trusted the great European brand names of the prewar era. Many of these companies are still flourishing: Prudential, Zurich, and Assicurazioni Generali, to name just three.

More than most families, Jewish families needed the security offered by what financial advisers today might call 'a diversified portfolio'. As they watched anti-Semitism mutate into open violence and persecution on the streets of Nazi Germany, Jews across Europe needed comprehensive insurance against an uncertain future.

Five decades into that future as the Swiss banks affair hit the headlines, seasoned Swiss diplomats and bankers were quick to remind their detractors of the comprehensive nature of financial protection. Defending their prior role as bankers to persecuted Jewish families Swiss executives sought to point the finger at other financial institutions equally compromised by the turmoil of the Nazi era. 'We were not the only ones put in a difficult position' became an increasingly familiar refrain at briefings and symposiums attended by Switzerland's ruling elite.

Nazi, Allied or neutral, every country in Europe harboured financial institutions which thrived in the chaos of war. Inside the

Reich every industrial and commercial enterprise was compromised to a greater or lesser degree. From the industrial giants such as Volkswagen to the corner store, the Nazi invasions across Europe changed the conditions of business and threw open opportunities that would never have occurred otherwise.

For miners and manufacturers the war created a boom in demand for manufactured goods. For financial institutions—like banks and insurance companies—the war meant many customers, particularly Jewish customers, were leaving funds which might never be reclaimed. For unscrupulous financiers the war years represented an exceptional opportunity to loot the accounts and policies of the dead or the doomed. This rampant looting of personal fortunes began inside Germany once the Nazis took power in 1933. In the early years it was done with a veneer of civility. Jewish families were ordered to hand over fortunes through arcane rules and regulations which represented no more than a smokescreen for government-sanctioned robbery. As the Nazis spread across Europe the process was repeated.

In the early years of the Reich highly formalised procedures were enacted against Jewish families with occasional attempts to provide 'compensation'. As the war extended into the 1940s this 'business as usual' facade began to disappear and in the end Jewish families were evicted on the spot with little pretence towards an ordered handover of family assets.

Within months of the Swiss banks scandal reaching its zenith in February 1997—when the issue graced the covers of both *Time* and *Newsweek* inside a fortnight—Jewish activists had broadened their range of initiatives to include legal moves against both non-Swiss banks and insurance companies throughout Europe.

The first class action on any issue related to Holocaust assets had been filed in New York almost a year earlier in October 1996 when Holocaust survivor Gizella Weisshaus sued the Swiss banking industry for $20 billion. The action led by New York lawyer Edward Fagan had received worldwide publicity as both the scale of the manoeuvre and the characters behind the case offered the public a tangible view of the Holocaust assets issue.

Gizella Weisshaus was a Romanian Jew from the town of Sighet who had fled to New York after the Holocaust. Her entire family had died during the Holocaust, and Weisshaus had somehow survived alone at Auschwitz. Her father had been a financier in prewar Romania and had told the family that he had deposited money in Swiss banks to care for their future. Weishauss was joined by 10 000 other claimants in the class action which created a major propaganda weapon for Fagan and other US advocates.

In the same period the World Council of Orthodox Jewish Communities filed a case against the big three Swiss banks— Credit Suisse, Swiss Bank Corporation and Union Bank of Switzerland—while another class action was filed in the Brooklyn Federal Court on behalf of five families living in the United States, Canada and Britain. And that was just the legal activity mounting against the Swiss banks.

In June 1997 the international insurance industry drew a breath when a Manhattan court received a class action which represented 10 000 people who had taken out insurance policies during the Second World War. Fourteen major European insurance companies were named in the action, which called for each company to pay $1 billion in compensation. Among the Swiss companies named were Rentenanstalt, Zurich and Baloise. Non-Swiss groups included were Italy's Assicurazioni Generali and Germany's Allianz. Separately, the Simon Wiesenthal Center in Los Angeles had launched a major indictment against Switzerland's Winterthur Insurance group, claiming that life insurance policies of people who had disappeared during the war had been paid out to a Swiss Government fiduciary by the insurer.

Later as part of a wider campaign against non-Swiss banks, Fernande Bodner, whose family had fled France for New York during the Nazi years, launched a class action naming some of the best known banks in Europe. The suit highlighted alleged activities of French banks such as Credit Lyonnais, Société Generale and Paribas during the Vichy regime of 1940–1944. It said the banks collaborated with the Nazis and the administration of Marshal Petain in 'plundering foreign exchange, securities, jewellery, art treasures and business enterprises'.

To the horror of British banking officials the suit also named Barclays Bank, which had twelve branches operating in Vichy, France. The suit claimed that Barclays was one of the key banks used by Nazi officials for holding the proceeds of looted property sales which had originally belonged to Jewish families.

The class actions drew a mixed response from both Jews and other factions involved in the Holocaust assets affair. Outside the United States there was a certain discomfort with this distinctly American style of highly adversarial legal dispute. Moreover, there was strong evidence that the class actions could put the brakes on the momentum that was being achieved in relation to the recovery of assets, particularly from Swiss banks under the Volcker Commission. Class actions, however, had proved powerful in the past, particularly where legal issues had a universal scope such as the legal battles over abuses by pharmaceutical and oil companies in the United States.

For Australia's significant but aging population of Holocaust survivors, broadening the Holocaust assets issue to include an investigation of other companies in addition to the Swiss banks made perfect sense. They could remember insurance brokers in the cities of prewar Europe selling life insurance policies to their parents. They also remembered that the Swiss were not alone in failing in their duties to the Jewish families. Before long it would become obvious that non-Swiss banks or insurance companies would prove little better than the Swiss when it came to dealing with Holocaust victims. Indeed they would regularly appear every bit as difficult as the Swiss Bankers Association at its most obstinate.

In the centre of Paris stretched between the Tuileries Gardens and the Place Vendome is the Rue de Castiglone. Here are found world-famous boutiques and hotels such as the Ritz which have made Paris a byword for elegance. The district has long been one of the most fashionable quarters of Paris and in the 1930s at number 12 on the Rue de Castiglone was located the Banque Des Pays De l'Europe Centrale.

The Banque Des Pays was a bank for the rich, a home away from home for the merchants and landed gentry of Central Europe who used Paris as a business base and a playground with equal enthusiasm. The big banks of Switzerland had established a reputation for harbouring international funds by the 1930s, but smaller banks all over Europe could also handle 'asset management' with skill and discretion. Banque Des Pays De l'Europe Centrale was one of these banks.

Once Paris was fully under Nazi control, the Nazis began to regularly loot properties and funds belonging to Jews. The Banque Des Pays, which specialised in foreign owned accounts, was a perfect target for the Germans. Among the bank's clients was Siegmund Friedmann, a Jewish banker and furniture manufacturer from the city of Czernovitz in north west Romania. He made a string of deposits, often in sterling, in the years before the war. By the time the war broke out Friedmann had more than 41 000 French francs in his account. Sometime in 1942 the Banque Du Pays received instructions to transfer 42 000 francs from Friedmann's account to the German Treasury.

When the war ended the Banque Des Pays returned to normal trading practices but in common with many banks across Europe it found some of its Jewish customers appeared to be missing. Siegmund Friedmann, for example, had died hungry and ridden with typhoid in a labour camp at Mogilev in Transnistria, which is now a part of the Ukraine.

In the 1920s anti-Semitism in Romania was driven by the feared Iron Guard which persecuted the country's prewar Jewish population of almost 750 000. It also surfaced with a vengeance inside the key student bodies.

In December 1927 Romania came to international attention when the students from the League of National Christian Defence led a pogrom in Orodea Mare. The pogrom itself was not so much the news as the fact that the government had subsidised it to the extent of providing the students with free train travel to Oradea Mare where they wrecked five synagogues and ignited rioting across the city.

The Friedmann family were to pay a high price for residing in the Romanian province of Buikovina where the pro-Nazi dictatorship of Marshal Ion Antonescu had replaced King Carol II in 1940.

Under a program known as 'Rumanianization' the Antonescu regime had moved thousands of Jews to the east; in the newly acquired state of Transnistria alone 96 000 out of 146 000 deported Jews would die during the war. More than 7000 Jews from Czernovitz were deported to Mogilev, a town across the Dniester River in northern Transnistria where starvation and disease awaited.

By the end of the war four out of ten Romanian Jews were killed, some in circumstances as grotesque as witnessed anywhere in the Reich. In Bucharest the January 1941 pogrom led by the Iron Guard saw 120 Jews murdered in the streets. In one part of the city the bodies of several murdered Jews were brought to a slaughterhouse and hung on meathooks with the legend 'kosher meat' scrawled on the walls.

Siegmund Friedmann's wife, Necha, and daughter, Erica, somehow avoided the murder squads which had roamed Romania. They had crossed the Dneister River unharmed and when they got to Mogilev a typhoid epidemic was raging but they would survive that too as Necha walked daily in the snow to sterilise her daughter's clothes. But the family could not avoid the machinations of the Third Reich in Paris more than a thousand miles away. Throughout the war they believed Siegmund's deposit at the Banque Des Pays would be waiting for them when the war was over.

Sitting in an anonymous office in North Sydney's business district Erica Turek still has disturbed memories from the Mogilev camp and the long trail of camps and orphanages that were to come in the years following the war. She explains:

My mother's life was turned totally upside down by the war. She had come from a bourgeois family and she had never even worked before when she found herself in a labour camp. Her family were grain merchants from Lvov in Poland and she had a comfortable life before the war.

In the 1930s two of my mother's brothers were sent to Vienna to study medicine. In those days women had a very set role in the order of things and my grandfather decided the brothers needed help in Vienna since they were living away from home for the first time. So my mother was sent off to join them and to keep the house running nice and tidy for her brothers. It was while she was in Vienna in the 1930s that she met my father Siegmund who used to travel to Austria on business.

My father was also from a bourgeois family, his family had a lot of interests in Romania around the city of Czernovitz [also known as Chernovtsky]. The family had a very well-known restaurant which specialised in fish, it is still remembered by the older people in the city.

With my Uncle Paul my father was well established in
business, they had a furniture factory and my father
was also the part owner and director of a bank. So he
knew banking intimately and he had dealings with banks
in both Zurich and Paris.

Erica was born on New Year's Day 1939 in the final months before
the outbreak of World War II. With the invasion of Poland in 1939
and the public expression of support for that action by the
Romanian Government, Jewish families in Romania realised that
life was about to become very difficult.

Necha Friedmann began to take precautions for the future,
among the most practical of these was her decision to continue to
breastfeed her nine-month-old daughter. She knew this would help
Erica survive whatever difficulties might face her in the coming
months. By the end of 1939 the Friedmann family had been
expelled from Czernovitz; together with grandparents, aunts and
uncles they were deported to the Ukraine.

We were sent to Mogilev which was supposed to be a
transit camp, but it was a concentration camp and we
were there for the entire duration of the war. It was
a dreadful place and my mother would tell me in later
years of the starvation and the cold. She showed a
strong ability to survive there that would surface
again and again in the future.

After the war my mother and I went back to
Czernovitz, I was still only six at this stage and my
mother returned to this devastated place. We stayed
with an aunt who had also survived and my mother tried
to make some money by trading salt.

Her life had changed so much from living in comfort
in Vienna and Czernovitz before the war to travelling
around the Romanian countryside in all weather trading
blocks of salt for blocks of butter. It was hard work
and very dangerous for a woman to be travelling around
by herself like that in the chaotic years immediately
after the war. During that time she tried to piece her
life together again and rebuild contact with her
family. My mother had come from a large family—there
was thirteen of them originally in Lvov. Three of them
had emigrated to America before the war and one of her

sisters had managed to get to Israel through Italy after the war broke out.

So she had plans to join her brothers in America and she tried writing to all the major Jewish agencies. She didn't have much luck, but she decided it was time to leave Romania and go somewhere else, anywhere appeared better than Romania at the time. We went to a displaced persons camp in Vienna where she had lived before the war. Here again there was a stream of letters over and back to America and she was making endless trips to various offices. All the time she had to mind me, we were by ourselves . . . the main thing I remember of this time is being alone and living in this huge barracks around a sort of military square and being found wandering alone at night. Oh yes . . . and I learned some Hebrew and my prize for doing so well was a cake of soap.

From Vienna we moved on to Paris. I remember travelling on the train and seeing American soldiers, on that train I had a Coca-Cola for the first time this was a big deal for a war child like me. I was very young so it's hard to get the sequence of events right, but around that time I had to stay in an orphanage where there was a serious fire one night and several of the children were badly burnt. It was very disturbing, I can still remember their screams when the bandages had to be changed.

In Paris my mother went to work in a factory, repairing silk stockings. I remember she just did not know what to do with me, I was alone in this little room a lot of the time, my mother was just working like a dog at all hours. It seemed like the city was full of war refugees working there trying to get visas to go somewhere else.   .

After some time my mother found that leaving me alone so much was not good for me and sent me to a Jewish 'boarding school' near Versailles. It was a boarding school of a special kind in that once again the children were nearly all orphans whose parents had perished during the Holocaust. My most memorable moment there was having to have my long hair cut off because we all got infected with lice.

It was during this time in Paris that my mother went back to the Rue de Castiglone and the Banque Des Pays De l'Europe Centrale and tried to recover the family money.

This was around 1948 and the bank had obviously survived the war in good condition because it was still trading in the centre of Paris. They sent my mother a letter which I still have in my possession which details my father's deposit of more than 40 000 francs. The letter also details various complications relating to the money, but looking back on it she must have been in such a strong position then if she only had known what to do. Of course she was penniless and powerless, she didn't have a chance against sophisticated Parisian bankers.

My mother desperately wanted to get into America. I think that is really where she was putting most of her efforts but the quota system locked us out, and she had no real chance of reuniting with her brothers. So she started to try for Australia even though she knew nothing about it and knew nobody here, in the end we got a visa and we arrived in Sydney with the help of the Jewish Welfare Society in 1950.

After disembarking at Sydney Harbour, Erica and Necha stayed for a short while at a hostel in Greenwich before moving to a one-bedroom flat in Coogee. Necha Friedmann had to quickly find a way to support herself and her daughter. Erica remembers:

Once again I was alone. To make ends meet my mother worked seven days a week. Although on Sundays she worked at home having brought home additional piece work. She did invisible mending, this was something she had picked up in Paris. I did most of the housework and our one big treat was a trip to the cinema on Saturday nights.

Later with a little help from her brothers in America we managed to move to a two-bedroom flat in Bondi Junction. After several years my mother managed to put a deposit on a terrace house in Bondi Junction and she ran it as a boarding house. Necha had a very hard life even when we got here to Australia.

I went to school during the week and still did most of the housework at weekends. When I was in my fourth year of high school it was decided that I should quit school and go to work, so I got my first job working in a lottery office as a clerk.

Then when I was nineteen I got married to Joseph

Turek, we had one daughter, Katherine. My mother died in 1975 but I did not discover the bank documents until 1993 when I was going through her papers. As part of an application I was making to the German Government for compensation, I found various items relating to the war years including the letter to her from Banque Des Pays De l'Europe Centrale.

The letter is dated 24 March 1948 and addressed to my mother at Rue Mayran in Paris. It was a big bank still in those days, in the headed notepaper it mentions the bank has share capital of 130 million francs. The letter very clearly mentions my father's account at the bank and details the total amount in the account as 41 895 francs. In today's values that is a lot of money. It is a sum worth fighting for and I am really only beginning to do that now. I saw all the coverage of the Swiss banks in 1997 and I decided that I should do something about my own situation.

I have started a process now which I hope will see this money returned. I have engaged Henry Burstyner and I think we will make progress in the current environment where governments and banks across Europe are reviewing their behaviour during and after the war.

It has not been the case that I have spent years regretting what life might have been like without this money. In fact my husband and I were pretty determined to get the most out of life after the bleakness of my childhood. We both worked very hard—I have spent most of my life working in personnel agencies—but we enjoyed our life too. Between 1973 and 1978 we had built a boat and we decided to sail around the world with Katherine doing her school by correspondence. We had more than four years living on the boat.

Today I still work every day and I also try to educate people about the world that people like me grew up in. But it is very difficult, I work regularly as a volunteer in the Sydney Holocaust Museum and I meet young Australians and it amazes how little they know about the Nazi years. Sometimes I wonder if they even know what I'm talking about, I wonder if they understand at all the pain and the anguish we went through.

I was robbed of my father, I was robbed of my grandparents, uncles, aunts, and cousins. I was robbed of my home, my childhood and my teenage years. While my peers were going to university or just plain enjoying themselves, I was washing clothes and sweeping floors. In fact, I was even robbed of my mother who had to work so hard to put food in our mouths that she had little time and even less energy for me.

None of these things can be given back to me. Only one thing—that money which was stolen by the bank from my family—can be returned. That is the least that can be given back to me. This is my right, both moral and legal, I ask only for justice and restitution.

Chapter six

A LOST WORLD

Sunday morning in the town of Oswiecim, south west of Krakov in southern Poland. It is the first week of spring and the sun is shining weakly on this sad little village, better known by the name the world associates with death and destruction—Auschwitz.

A sub-zero wind is blowing along the tree-lined road that leads from the town to its two infamous camps—Auschwitz and Birkenau—which are set about one kilometre apart. The road is dotted with old factories that have seen better times. The only sign that they are still in use are the rows of little beaten-up cars in the carparks.

It is coming up ten o'clock and the tour groups and tourists who visit the death camps all year round are nowhere to be seen. Instead most people in this provincial Catholic village are getting ready for mass.

As worldwide debate continues to rage over how to commemorate the Holocaust, the authorities in Oswiecim have a delicate task in guiding visitors around the death camps. Any hint of promoting the town on the back of its horrific past will only bring the wrath of the international community, while any suggestion the town is forgetting its history will also be condemned. As a result Oswiecim has tried to compromise; there are some signs for the camp but not enough of them. They simply say, 'museum', offering no further information except an arrow pointing the visitor in the appropriate direction.

Turning right off this tree-lined avenue the road leads up to Birkenau, where in the later stages of the war the Nazis were killing 10 000 people a day. At Birkenau, a vast and windy site with its sentry posts and fencing still intact, it is eerily quiet. A small herd of deer is walking almost silently between the ruins of the gas chambers. They come in from the forests which surround the camp, no more than a few hundred metres away.

Back down the road at Auschwitz a mini-bus pulls up with one of the first visiting groups of the day. It is a class of Jewish schoolboys who walk into the main reception building with their teacher. Some of the boys look solemn, some look like typical schoolboys on a day tour; they are talking excitedly to one another. The teachers look nervous. Children under thirteen are 'not advised' to enter the camp. These boys might be fifteen at the most.

Inside the camp two middle-aged men are walking towards the

low door of a crematorium. Both deep in reflection they accidentally walk into each other as they move to enter the chamber. Embarrassed they both try to let the other through first, their civility seems almost theatrical in a place of such barbarity.

At the sterilisation ward two women are climbing the stairs back towards the front door. They have walked up from the streaked floors and the dun-coloured walls where women like themselves sat shivering in rags, reluctant guinea pigs for the grotesque regime which ruled this site 50 years ago.

As they leave the building a truck from one of the nearby factories on the main road blows its horn. The sound shatters the silence inside the camp. The relief on hearing this everyday noise of the town outside is almost palpable on the faces of these two visitors.

Once the pride and joy of Poland, the region of Silesia is now a rust belt; a landscape of coal and steel which the world no longer needs.

Poland is enjoying its most prosperous era since the 1920s as GDP rates top 7 per cent per annum and inflation stays within control.

Foreign investment is pouring in as the country maintains strong growth rates. The Polish zloty is no longer a second-rate currency and international investors are viewing the country as a gateway to the untapped resources of neighbouring Belarus and the Ukraine. Warsaw is booming, foreign hotels are opening up and apartment blocks are under construction throughout the city. In Warsaw's best restaurants, the professional classes are eating American-style meals and driving home in limousines or fashionable jeeps.

But the new money is not pouring into Silesia. The government is trying everything to boost the region, special economic incentives are offered to those who will venture south and help the region adapt to a global economy where the microchip not the smelter is the secret of success.

Back in its heyday, Silesia, the southernmost region of Poland, could rival the Ruhr in Germany or the 'black country' in the English Midlands for its productivity and grim prosperity. Among those who thrived in this climate was the extended family of Siegmund Siegreich.

'Irrepressible' is perhaps the best word to describe Siegmund Siegreich. In November 1941 shortly after being sent to his first camp, Skarzysko-Kamienna in central Poland, Siegmund escaped his captors and spent the freezing winter of 1941–1942 with the Polish underground in the woods around the town of Sandomierz. Recaptured by the Nazis after four months on the run he avoided execution by using an assumed name. Since the Nazis were unaware he was an escapee he was sent to camp again; by coincidence he was sent back to Skarzysko-Kamienna.

The camp served as a slave labour centre for the massive German armaments plants which dotted the region. The work carried out by prisoners involved dealing with metal and chemicals in the most brutal circumstances imaginable. It is estimated that about 30 000 Jews entered the gates of the camp and around 23 000 never survived, dying of exhaustion, disease and starvation.

On 1 July 1944 Siegmund was evacuated from Skarzysko-Kamienna and transferred to Czestochowa camp where he spent the rest of the war. He was liberated by the Russian Army on 17 January 1945.

Siegmund's great-grandfather, also named Siegmund Siegreich had founded the Eltes Group, a diversified industrial conglomerate which produced a range of industrial supply products including calcium and fireclay. The factory was one of the biggest in Silesia employing about 10 000 workers. The fortune made by his great-grandfather ensured the family were securely placed among Poland's Jewish bourgeoisie, and each succeeding generation had also entered industry with varying success.

Siegmund's maternal grandfather, David Siegreich had also shone in industrial circles, building Sigma Ltd, a successful dye-producing factory in Welnowiec which employed more than a thousand workers. The plant specialised in the production of aniline, a new product at the time which allowed dyes of brilliant colours to be produced cheaply. Sigma supplied textile and leather plants in Poland and also carried on some export work with factories in the United Kingdom including the Williams Hounslow group.

The factory was most probably 'acquired' during the war by IG Farben, the German chemicals giant which manufactured Zyklon B, the gas used to kill Jews in Auschwitz and other death camps.

Known today almost solely for Zyklon B, IG Farben was in fact the industrial heart of the Reich. One of Europe's most powerful companies in the 1930s, the extent of IG Farben's dealings with the Nazis is still coming to light. But it is known that no company was more instrumental in exploiting the Nazi era than the giant conglomerate. At Auschwitz the group built a synthetic oil and rubber plant, and then aided the Nazis in designing the death camp in the most efficient way possible. Among IG Farben's employees at Auschwitz was Josef Kramer, the notorious 'Beast of Belsen'.

One of IG Farben's main routes to enrichment in World War II was by taking over factories in occupied territories. In the case of the Siegreich family's Sigma factory, it seems the group did not even trouble themselves to evaluate the business as a going concern; it simply ransacked the plant for machinery and components; by the time Germany's most famous industrial conglomerate was finished raiding Sigma of its assets, there was nothing left in Welnowiec but a derelict shell of building. After the war a former caretaker at Sigma told Siegmund the plant and machinery at the factory had been removed and sent back to Germany by IG Farben.

Separately, Siegmund's own father Samuel ran a timber and building materials supply business in the city of Katowice, while both Siegmund's parents were entitled to a share in wider family business interests. As Siegmund explains:

My family were very involved in business and there was a lot of connections between the extended family and its various business concerns. But my father had his own operations quite separate to the Sigma factory and this was basically a building supplies business. It was largely timber supply to steel mills and mines in the region.

I have been able to re-establish quite a lot of detail about this timber business and it is the centre of one of my claims which is against Dresdner Bank, a bank which is still one of the most successful banks in Germany today. [Dresdner Bank received an operating licence in Australia in January 1998].

Immediately after the war broke out the Germans took the timber business off my parents and they were sent to the ghetto, they would later die in the camps, I don't even know which one. However, you must remember that in the first months of the Nazi occupation things were not so bad. There was this impression they made that they would make small monthly payments to my parents for losing their business.

But the payments ceased very quickly. The authorities
took over the timber yards almost immediately and
appointed a *Treuhander* [literally translated as a faithful
hand, a Nazi manager] to manage the business. Within a few
months they decided to liquidate the business and transfer
the proceeds of the liquidation to an account at Dresdner
Bank.

In the 1960s I tracked down this *Treuhander*, Ernst Waida,
in Germany. He signed an affidavit supporting my claim.
Waida said the proceeds of the liquidation had come to 200
000 reichmarks which had been lodged in the Dresdner Bank.
He also said the price achieved reflected the fact the
Nazis were selling off the stock very cheaply.

Not many people have been able to resurrect the sort of
evidence I have completed now against Dresdner Bank. I
made some serious efforts to tackle the bank with a
solicitor in 1971 but they said the account had been
transferred to Dresden which was in East Germany and they
would have nothing to do with it. But now I believe we
have a chance to re-open this case, the division between
East and West Germany is gone and this bank is thriving as
far as I can see. I have engaged a solicitor in the town
of Worms to work on the case for me.

Dresdner Bank is supposed to be re-examining its role in
the war so we are hopeful, I am talking about a claim now
of around 3 million marks against Dresdner Bank.[1]

At an international conference on Holocaust assets held in London in
December 1997, senior officials of Dresdner Bank pledged to re-open
the bank's wartime files, after Dresdner Bank and Deutsche Bank were
singled out as possible recipients of stolen gold during the Nazi era.

In March 1998 solicitors for Siegmund Siegreich located a
Dresdner Bank statement from 6 January 1945 relating to an
account held by his father's company at Katowice. The balance was
just 78 reichsmarks.

Siegmund's ability to establish an account, however small, at
Dresdner Bank has been a breakthrough. He is now looking for a
similar breakthrough in a parallel action against the Italian insurer
Assicurazioni Generali which is being handled by his nephew,
Yedida Goren, a solicitor in Israel.

Siegmund's father Samuel had an insurance policy with the
Assicurazioni Generali when he lived in Katowice. In the same way

Abraham Siegreich (bottom right) Ruth Crane's resourceful uncle who was behind several schemes to protect the family. Courtesy Ruth Crane

Arthur Shafir at age fifteen. During this period his family was living in Gryzbow, the Warsaw hardware district. Courtesy Arthur Shafir

Dr David Castelan with his aunt Irma Selzer. Working together they led the family's campaign to retrieve city properties in Berlin. Courtesy David Castelan

Inner courtyard of the Castelan buildings in Berlin today. The family had used the complex for domestic apartments and as a garments factory. Courtesy David Castelan

The Castelan family's canalside property in Berlin's fashionable Postrasse district.
Courtesy David Castlean

Leo Lippmann in his Hamburg home before the war. His coin collection was later stolen by the Nazis. Courtesy Kurt Lippmann

Hendrik and Mina Grootemarsisk (right); taken outside Lemeleveld Farm before the war. Courtesy Martin Moen

Hendrik and Mina Grootemarsisk in 1980. Forty years after showing exceptional bravery in hiding Erica Deen on their farm. Courtesy Martin Moen

From left: Srulek, Hillel and Jakob Perlmutter. Srulek would later die in a Nazi 'hospital' where medical experiments were being carried out near Buchenwald. Courtesy Hillel Perlmutter

Hillel Perlmutter now lives in retirement in Sydney after a lifetime in the textile industry. His concentration camp number A5607 remains on his forearm. Courtesy Hillel Perlmutter

Krystyna Hugon at home on Sydney's north shore, she has never returned to Poland where she survived the Warsaw ghetto. Courtesy Krystyna Hugon

Krystna playing with Boghdan Kaczorowski—the Kaczorowski family risked execution by the Nazis in protecting a Jewish child. Courtesy Krystyna Hugon

The commercial buildings in central Warsaw which are currently under claim by Krystyna Hugon. The property has been fully restored by multinational companies. Courtesy the author

Henry Burstyner in his St Kilda office. The Melbourne lawyer has now achieved two significant settlements with the Swiss banking industry.
Courtesy *The Weekend Australian*/Graham Crouch

that Siegmund Siegreich made an unsuccessful attempt to deal with Dresdner Bank in the 1960s, he also tried to seek restitution from Assicurazioni Generali during that period only to be told he was wasting his time.

Based in Trieste, Assicurazioni Generali has been one of the Europe's biggest insurance groups since the beginning of the century; the group's current operations stretch from Ireland to Israel.

In the intervening years Assicurazioni Generali has gone from strength to strength but the past links between the company and wartime fascists regularly comes back to haunt the group. In the immediate fallout of the Holocaust assets affair in Italy, the Italian daily newspaper, *Corriere Della Sera*, broke the news that Assicurazioni Generali had insured concentration camps.

In late 1997 Siegreich came across an article from the *Jerusalem Post* dealing with the proposed takeover of Israel's biggest insurance group, Migdal Ltd, by none other than Assicurazioni Generali of Trieste. In Israel the US$300 million sale of Migdal had created an uproar with protesters rallying against the sale of a Jewish institution to a group which had outstanding Holocaust claims. Israel's Bank Leumi, which owned Migdal, would eventually push the deal through in February 1997 but not before the intervention of the Israeli Parliament, the Knesset.

Senior members of the Knesset's Finance Committee reached an agreement with Amihud Ben-Porat, Assicurazioni Generali's legal representative in Israel, that the company would not go ahead with its Migdal transaction without re-examining all Holocaust-era files. Throughout 1997 and 1998 Israeli politicians continued to put pressure on the Italian insurer with little public success. In June 1997 the issue flared again when a Knesset subcommittee threatened an insurance boycott on Migdal from government and public bodies.

In a bitter outburst the Knesset Finance Committee Chairman Avraham Ravitz said the negotiations with Migdal had been 'disgusting' and the group, now owned by the Italian insurer, had so far failed to hold itself to any of its written or verbal commitments on Holocaust-era accounts.[2]

Now in his seventies, Siegreich is waging two parallel campaigns against distant financial institutions. During his long life he has known these institutions better than most of his neighbours in Melbourne might realise—he spent ten years in Migdal's home base of Israel in the 1950s and a further decade in Dresdner Bank's home market of Germany in the 1960s.

In both cases a financial institution has made a major commitment to re-open its wartime records 50 years after Jewish account holders lost their fortunes in the tumult of war. Against both companies Siegreich has an exceptionally strong case: in the life insurance claim he has the family name of the account holder; in the bank dispute he has an affidavit signed by the depositor at Dresdner Bank. He has received no help from any Australian Government agency or any other official source and is financing the search for his family's lost assets out of his own pocket.

> Sometimes people ask me: 'How did your family ever get itself into such a position?' They say, 'Your parents were wealthy and they must have seen trouble coming.' But no one could have seen what was coming.
>
> I was fifteen in 1939 so I can remember things quite well. Poland was their home, in late 1939 they were in the middle of building an apartment block and a new house for themselves, it was not that easy to walk away.[3]

One of the most contentious problems facing both Holocaust survivors and bureaucrats at the centre of the Holocaust claims drama is the burden of proof. At one extreme, banks and insurers consistently asked for death certificates from Holocaust-era claimants, knowing only too well that death certificates were never issued at death camps.

On the other hand, there is little doubt that a small minority of inquiries sent to the Swiss banks and other financial institutions since the affair exploded in 1997 have been bogus. The Sydney office of Ernst and Young received inquiries from the most unlikely sources, often with little evidence to back up their interest.

The bogus claims exacerbate the already difficult and painful process undertaken by those claimants who have lost money, property and other valuables following the Second World War but do not possess any material evidence to substantiate their stories. Among the thousands of Holocaust survivors who remain in this position is Ruth Crane, who has been frustrated by the dormant accounts process. What makes her story so poignant is that her cousin, Siegmund Siegreich, would have been in an identical position if he did not possess the evidence he has collected from the Nazi-installed factory manager who took over his family business.

Siegmund and Ruth are now in their seventies. In prewar Poland they were two privileged children from a leading Silesian merchant family. Like Siegmund, Ruth managed to survive several concentration camps and after a period of dislocation in Europe and Israel she came to Australia. Unlike Siegmund, however, Ruth has neither the resources nor the energy to fully explore her right to restitution from the forces who took away her family and her fortune.

I was born Ruth Siegreich on the 22 November 1927 in the town of Siemianowice. I came from a large extended Jewish family who had business interests throughout the region. My father Julek and mother Zosia were very loving and my sisters, Lilka and Carmela, and me all felt very loved and very comfortable in our house as children. The family had been timber merchants in the region for generations, there were timber yards, and a timber mill and forests. My family were always talking about business and banking. They would sit around the dining table in the evening speaking about the affairs of the day, and as a child I was of course listening in to these conversations. We lived very comfortably in an apartment with quite a few staff, I remember different people helping us . . . a driver, a cook and a woman who used to do the washing.

Every summer for about six weeks we would go to my grandfather's house on my mother's side. They had a wonderful large house, it is still there today in Sulejow. We had lovely long holidays in that house.

Also during the year on almost every Sunday we would have big family gatherings in Bendzin where my paternal grandparents lived. Here I would play with all my cousins including Siegmund [Siegreich], who now lives not far from me in Melbourne. Living close to the German border, we witnessed the distress which Jewish families were experiencing in Germany, and we talked often to Jewish refugees fleeing from the Nazis.

We were painfully aware of the enormous suffering which these German Jews were enduring and it alerted my father to make provisions for our security.

My father went abroad on a business trip in 1938, which was a very auspicious time if you think about it. I remember clearly because my mother who was not used to him being away had to take over running the business.

Then not very long after he came back from the trip he came and said to me very carefully that I would always be provided for. He said that my children, even my grandchildren, would be able to live comfortably because he had put money away for us. He said the money was safe and secure abroad. The family always trusted my father—his wisdom and his business sense.

My father did a lot of his business together with his younger brother Abraham. He was an exceptionally able man, and though he was quite young then in the 1930s, he was already running a business for my grandparents.

There was a lot of talk in our house about making provision for the future as Nazi power began to grow across Europe. Still we were really surprised just how fast the Nazis took over the country, it seemed like overnight we were being ordered to leave Siemianowice. I remember Abraham came over to my parents house and they were very quickly sorting out documents and banknotes and burning some documents before they left.

After being evicted from our homes, my immediate family and grandparents and some of my relations all assembled in the town. But within a very short period of time it was decided that my parents would go ahead of the rest of the family to Russia. There was this plan that the family could all go to Russia and stay there until the war blew over. My father had business connections all across the eastern part of Poland who he knew would help us on our journey. So we left the mill in a horse-drawn cart one night, and we travelled by night only for most of the next week. Eventually we were smuggled across the Russian border. But we were not inside Russia very long—maybe only a few days—when my parents decided they had made a big mistake and they should go back to Poland.

They sort of convinced themselves that the Nazi regime would not be so bad, the Germans had not been that bad when they took over our region of Poland in the First World War and people just wanted to believe that maybe this time they might not be too severe. But more than that my parents had principles which they wanted to retain despite the war. They had responsibilities to their home place and that meant a lot to them.

Around the end of December 1939 we settled down in the town of Olkusz, which is not far from the city of Bendzin. Shortly after we got back my father and Abraham were ordered by the Germans to help the *Treuhander* to run our old timber mill. In Olkusz we had a relation, Josef Plockier, who was living a very dangerous life, he was masquerading as a German officer. This was an extraordinary thing to do, but in times of war extraordinary things happen.

Josef had German papers and he was a wonderful man for my family, and on the 30th of July 1940 he saved my father's life when a whole group of Jewish men were executed in the town. It was through Josef's connections that my father was not included. In fact, Josef saved us many times in the Olkusz ghetto by diverting soldiers and giving orders to guards that ensured our survival. Around the end of 1942 he was discovered by the authorities and they killed him immediately.

When they liquidated the Olkusz ghetto in June 1942 people were lined up and taken away to the camps. We were put in a line-up and I remember my father carrying me on his shoulders. But once again there was some influence working for us behind the scenes because someone spirited us away from the thousands of people being lined up in the city and shortly afterwards we were moved to Bendzin.

Abraham was behind this rescue in Olkusz. He had made arrangements with people, most likely the *Treuhander*, offering future payments so that we could get away.

Sometime in December we were back in another line-up. This was a horrific day, they were tearing families apart, killing women and children. We were all assembled in the square called Umszalg Place and the Nazi soldiers were there picking people at random, making sure they filled their quotas for the camps.

For the second time we were somehow spared during this line-up and we continued to live in Bendzin, but about seven weeks later I was caught and put to work in a clothing factory making uniforms for the Nazis. It was not too bad there but I was only in the factory a few weeks when there was a round-up and this time I was trapped. I remember trying to hide behind this line of uniforms but I was seen and they made me join the round-up for the labour camps. It was the beginning of a dreadful time, I was to go through four different camps in the next few years.

In Oderberg, which was my first camp, I was introduced to the awful life we would have to endure in the future. I later found out that while I was in Oderberg my parents had made a very serious effort to get out of Poland even though it was very late in the war by then—1943—they had good connections through Abraham. They had managed to get Swiss passports and they had an arrangement to go to Switzerland, this was their second attempt to escape.

This is what convinces me they had money in the Swiss banks. They were going to Switzerland and they had already said there was money abroad. I never really thought about it then, but now I think about it a great deal. There are funds there that could make my life and the lives of my children and grandchildren easier.

Not very long after I arrived in Oderberg I nearly died when I got an infection which made me very ill. It was really serious and anywhere else it would have required an operation, but if you were sick in the camp, you had no chance of survival, so I couldn't let them know I was ill. My friends took terrible risks for me, standing in for me during roll calls and covering my tracks. But I was so ill I needed help. They found another inmate who was a doctor, Dr Deutsch. He had been a top surgeon at a hospital in Vienna and now he was in this camp. He said he would help me, but he had nothing to work with except a penknife.

I remember Dr Deutsch so well, he was a young man, we were all young, he stood there with his penknife and he said to me, 'If you survive this you will be famous in the medical journals.'

They made a makeshift table for me and he used the penknife to cut me open. It was terrible, I had horrible pain and the infection just poured out of my body. I was in agony and hiding all the time trying to recover, occasionally one of the girls got me hot water which offered some relief to me. Slowly I recovered, I just don't know how I did.

When I look back I think as young girls in those conditions we had a lot of spiritual strength, and there was this tremendous innocence. I think that is what got us through. Despite everything a memory comes to the fore of the camp inmates and their never diminishing will to live, they had an abundance of courage and hope.

I was in camps all through the rest of the war, the Germans always kept us moving around. After Oderberg I was in Seibersdorf, then Blechamer and finally Peterswaldau where I was liberated in May 1945. By the time the Russians came into Peterswaldau I was just a number; my name was 26748.

I remember going back to Siemianowice on the train, I had to make so many decisions and the whole situation was such a shock. I had to cope with my feelings, or my lack of feelings might be a more accurate way to describe the time.

You know in Siemianowice there was 500 Jewish children in the town and by the end of the war there was three. I was one of the three children, the other two were brothers; they left and went to live in Los Angeles.

On the train back to Siemianowice I had met a man and we became very good friends. This was my late husband Maurice, he died in 1994. He too was coming out of the camps and making an attempt to go back to his homeplace. Only nine months after we met on the train we were married.

Poland was in chaos when we went back after the war, people moving all over the place, people trying to rebuild their lives. There was nobody there for me, all I could find was an old neighbour who tried to tell me what had occurred during the war. I was not even eighteen and in complete turmoil, money was the last thing on my mind, but when I look back at it that was a crucial time before the communists took over everything.

Everyone else in my family group had perished in the war. They were all killed at Auschwitz. I was, and still am, broken-hearted about this. I survived in the camps because I was useful and I had an inner strength, it was a strength we shared among ourselves in those places.

My family would still have had business operations and houses in Siemianowice when I went back, but I was not thinking along those lines. Maurice and I had a plan to go to Palestine and we joined an Aliyah Bet. We walked all the way across Europe with no papers or anything to get to Israel. I remember walking huge distances over mountains, and crossing rivers with this group.

Eventually we got to a harbour in Italy where the idea was we would travel by sea to Haifa. The crossing between Italy and Israel was very difficult. The ship was terrible, everybody was on top of each other. When we were out at sea the ship was stopped by a British Navy vessel and we were taken to Cyprus.

We ended up in this displaced persons camp for more than a year, just waiting for someone to make a decision on our future. Then I remember Prince Charles was born on 14 November 1948 and they announced an amnesty and we were able to travel to Israel.

We got to Israel at the end of that year just as the state was being formed. We were there for nearly two years. I suppose it was in Israel that I got my first indication of the long-term damage that had been done to me in the camps. I wanted to have a child, and I got pregnant but I was very ill and in the eighth month I had a miscarriage. After the miscarriage I was told by a specialist that there was no way I could try and have another child.

Things were pretty tough where we lived, in Kfav-Saba, there was very little there. All sorts of food was hard to get, and the supply of even basic goods was very poor but I loved Israel and I always will.

My husband had a sister in Melbourne, and we decided to give Australia a try in 1951. I think we were in Melbourne a few weeks and I remember walking down a street saying to myself, this is so good, so free. I loved it straightway and I always will. A lot of things came right in Australia, I had a boy and a girl despite what the doctors had told me. My little girl was 1 pound 14 ounces when she was born, but she survived.

For all my life I never thought about the family's interests in Poland, for me Poland was the past I just could not face thinking about that time. I feel it is only in the last year or two that I can face it. In fact I am planning to make a trip to Poland with my son. I know there is property there that I am entitled to, I remember that my parents paid 40 000 szloty for a building in 1926, that was a lot of money then. We owned those buildings and they were taken from us. There were funds too in Switzerland, I am entitled to that and my family are entitled to it.[4]

Siegmund Siegreich and Ruth Crane are among thousands of Jews who originated from Silesia before the war. As a thriving industrial region in the 1920s and 1930s the district has more than its fair share of lost fortunes. Investigations into the fate of Jewish assets in wartime Silesia can throw up remarkable outcomes but few have more resonance than the story of Zypora Frank, a British-based schoolteacher.

Zypora spent her childhood in Israel, where her parents would regularly refer obliquely to their lost properties in Silesia, in the district of Chrzanov. Her parents had spent the war in a Siberian labour camp. Afterwards they returned briefly to Silesia and tried to start a new life, but the atrocities of the recent past had poisoned the region for her family and they left for London. Her parents were never keen to talk about the war years, they had built new lives and resisted all temptation to examine their past in any detail.

By the late 1980s Zypora was a schoolteacher in her fifties with a strong interest in history, particularly that of her own family in Poland. In 1987 she volunteered to join a group of teachers travelling to Auschwitz. Zypora wanted to see the district her parents had fled during the war. She also wanted to find out what— if anything—the family had left unclaimed in Poland.

When she told her parents of her plans she was stunned—her father forbade her to travel to Silesia. Zypora was puzzled not at her parents anguish over Poland but at the intensity of their desire to protect her from the past. Slowly they relented to her wishes and produced a folio of documents and titles relating to prewar Poland.

As the story unfolded Zypora realised the family had been prosperous merchants in Chrzanov. Her grandfather had been a partner in a tile factory on the road from Oswiecim to Chrzanov. The title on the family's land at Chrzanov was clear; Zypora's mother had re-established the family's rights to properties on the village property register in the brief period when the family had tried to settle in Poland after the war.

While Zypora was in the process of investigating the Polish property titles her parents died from age-related illnesses and whatever could be established as her family property fell due to Zypora and her brother.

In 1998 *The Guardian* newspaper in England reported that Zypora and her brother had established their property holdings, but it had taken almost ten years for them to tell the wider world their family's terrible story. The Nazis had built Auschwitz camp on land owned by Zypora's grandfather between the smoky tile factories on the road leaving Oswiecim.

'When I found I owned part of Auschwitz it overtook my whole life,' she explained. 'I went to pieces.'[5]

Chapter seven

WHEN THE GOING
GETS TOUGH…

For Holocaust survivors such as Siegmund Siegreich, Ruth Crane or Zypora Frank, the whirlwind of activity surrounding Holocaust assets in early 1997 rekindled long-repressed hopes and desires that somehow they might retrieve some vestige of the world they had left behind in Eastern Europe.

Such hopes were echoed by tens of thousands of Jews around the globe as the Swiss Government and even the Swiss banks appeared ready to make major concessions to victims of the Holocaust. Among the major Jewish action groups such as the World Jewish Congress and the Simon Wiesenthal Center a view was shared that if the Swiss could be made to behave responsibly then national governments and major financial corporations across Europe would follow their example.

As the temperature of the debate rose to new levels it quickly became obvious the contest between the peak representative groups of worldwide Jewry and Switzerland's elite corps of bureaucrats and bankers would not be without casualties.

In the United States the battle was being led by the redoubtable Senator D'Amato, whose abrasive personal style did little to endear him to the Swiss. D'Amato is open to criticism for his handling of the heirless assets affair. His marshalling of circumstantial historical evidence to suit his means has often been aggressive in the extreme. Innocent Swiss citizens, particularly the families of Swiss lawyers identified on his 'lists of lawyers said to be hiding Jewish assets' were regularly maligned and mistreated. But D'Amato made waves and he was regularly getting results from his high-profile New York hearings of the Senate Banking Commission.

His approach was to barge through the veneer of civility which had bogged down Swiss–Jewish negotiations over dormant accounts for decades. Where Jewish leaders had previously tried to negotiate with the Swiss behind closed doors, the Senator preferred to burst through the door shouting demands at his adversaries.

D'Amato was never going to be easily pleased. In October 1997 as the Swiss banks waited for a pat on the back for releasing the first list of dormant accounts, D'Amato was publicly fuming over the pace of the SBA's claims procedures. The Senator was also indignant that despite spending millions on a worldwide public relations campaign the SBA had not yet given a cent back to anyone on the lists.

'The Swiss banks have lost all credibility,' barked the Senator in a public letter to the President of the SBA, George Krayer.[1] For the bankers of Zurich and Basel the loud-mouthed American politician was a major problem, the Swiss preferred more subtle methods. In the coming months they would respond in kind to the Senator's manoeuverings.

But first the SBA decided to dig itself into a deeper public relations hole by fumbling over the future of Christoph Meili. Instead of showing grace under pressure UBS appeared vindictive when they sacked Meili for breaching bank secrecy laws. Even inside Switzerland, the famously diplomatic leaders of the Jewish community were appalled at the insensitivity shown by UBS.

Sigi Feigel, the honorary president of the Jewish community in Zurich, explains: 'they were investigating a security guard who came upon this incident, instead of investigating who it was that had been shredding the documents at this critical juncture in relations between the Swiss banks and the Jewish community'.[2]

Sitting in his book-lined offices off the Bahnhofstrasse surrounded by pictures of his meetings with foreign dignitaries over the last five decades, Feigel is the definitive voice of the Swiss Jewry. He has been assertive at key moments in the Holocaust assets debate while always retaining a diplomatic balance between the interests of the wider Jewish diaspora and the interests of Switzerland. From Feigel's perspective trust is the key factor which needs to be built and preserved between the Jewish community and the Swiss banking system. However the fallout of the Meili incident ensured that trust between these two groups would be a long time coming.

Meili was a 23-year-old security guard who didn't have any idea what he was walking into when he blew the whistle on the Swiss banks. As UBS mused over whether it would lay charges against him for breaching bank secrecy, the world press waited for judgment. In this charged atmosphere Meili was way out of his depth and sorely in need of professional advice.

Indeed there was no lack of support or advice from activists both inside and outside the Jewish community; D'Amato himself offered the now unemployed security guard a job in the United States. But instead Meili came under the wing of Edward Fagan, perhaps the most aggressive lawyer ever to cross the door of a Swiss bank.

Fagan was already a controversial character. A key figure in a $20 billion class action against the Swiss banks out of New York, he now announced he had a new client, Christoph Meili, whose case he was taking as top priority.

As it turned out the Swiss would later close the case against Meili on the basis that the documents he recovered were too old to be covered by banking secrecy legislation. But that was never going to placate a New York lawyer; in early 1998 Fagan announced that Meili would sue UBS for US$2.6 billion in compensation.

The claim was structured so that $60 million would go to Meili and $2.5 billion would be 'redistributed to the Swiss population'. Fagan and a slightly bewildered looking Christoph Meili were on the evening news across the world within hours. It was a great story for the networks but a strategic setback for the majority of claimants. Jewish lobbyists could no longer claim exclusive rights to the moral high ground. Greed was appearing on both sides of the debate.

Meili's and Fagan's questionable tactics were topped off by a second legal manoeuvre by Charles Sonabend. Sonabend's parents had died at Auschwitz after having been turned away like at least 30 000 other Jews from the Swiss border during the war. The essence of Sonabend's claim was that he wanted 100 000 Swiss francs in compensation for damages for his parents illegal expulsion from Switzerland more than 50 years earlier. 'It pains me to put such a small price on my parents' life but this is what my lawyer has advised me,' he told a throng of news reporters.[3]

The British Broadcasting Corporation added further tensions to the debate by releasing its groundbreaking 'Nazi Gold' documentary. The program was shown around the world; in Australia it was presented as a 'Four Corners' special on the ABC. It was an excellent dissection of the major issues involved in the Holocaust assets debate. But in trying to add new material to the body of work already completed on Switzerland's wartime activities, the program accused Switzerland of allowing trainloads of Jews bound for death camps to pass through the country during the war. If hard evidence exists of this activity it was not shown in the documentary.

Within weeks of its release, the producers were mired in controversy. In Germany the cable broadcaster in the city of Kreuzlingen decided to stop carrying all BBC programs in protest at the documentary. The British Foreign Office then entered the debate to distance itself from the documentary. Inside Switzerland the program also triggered the first stirrings of a grassroots counterattack by Swiss citizens against what they saw as a smear campaign against their country's good name.

A group of Swiss citizens led by a member of Parliament sued the BBC for racist propaganda. The plaintiffs said the film would make people hate Switzerland—their claim was based on Switzerland's race laws.

As Switzerland underwent an international inquisition, the dormant accounts issue was raised in a number of countries around the world in mid 1997. In Australia it was established that no less than A$75 million is sitting in dormant accounts with the major Australian banks. Several accounts are worth more than A$100 000. The accounts are managed by the federal government once they have been transferred by commercial banks. The accounts are not secret, they are conventional accounts which for some reason retain unclaimed funds. The Australian Government publishes the entire list of all monies each year in a pamphlet called 'Have we got your money?'.

In contrast, researchers in Israel found the Israeli Government were not quite so forthcoming on dormant accounts and other heirless assets inside the state which housed the greatest number of Holocaust survivors in the world. But these assets had not been publicised. Israel's current affairs magazine *Jerusalem Report* reported that there were 11 000 unclaimed assets held by the Israeli Government. The magazine showed the government had never advertised the fact that more than 1000 apartments, 3200 parcels of land and more than 8000 deposits in a string of Israeli banks were unclaimed.

For the Swiss these findings were much needed ballast in the debate over Holocaust assets. To this day it is very rare indeed when a Swiss banker gets through an entire interview with a journalist or a historian without mentioning Israel's behaviour in relation to its own dormant accounts.

As 1997 opened, divisions also started to appear in the Jewish diaspora's approach to the issue of Holocaust assets. The World Council of Orthodox Jewish Communities, which represents one of the biggest groups of Holocaust survivors, said in mid January that it wished to distance itself from the inflammatory rhetoric that had recently been used by some Jewish organisations.[4] However, the momentum for action on Holocaust assets was now unstoppable.

In New York, the city's Comptroller General Alan Hevesi barred Union Bank of Switzerland from participating in a billion dollar New York City bond offering. A month later he was followed by the Massachusetts State Treasurer Joseph Malone, who terminated Massachusetts' short-term borrowing's contracts with UBS.

In Washington D'Amato was no longer the only senator putting his weight behind the push against Swiss banks. Late in 1997 Mike DeWine of Ohio and Patrick Moynihan of New York put forward a 'Nazi War Crimes Disclosure Act' proposal. The senators claimed the public interest overruled all other concerns when dealing with banks including Swiss banks. These bipartisan moves by US politicians against the Swiss banks sent shudders through the corridors of Zurich and Basel. Over the months that followed the Swiss banking industry realised the issue was more alive than ever before. Yet it would still take a long time before the major Swiss banks began to show any real sign of contrition for the actions of

their staff during World War II.

Switzerland's central bank, the Swiss National Bank, had bought Nazi gold with scant regard for the morality of trading with the enemy. The Bank for International Settlements in Basel had traded regularly with the Nazis, and commercial banks throughout Switzerland had taken deposits from thousands of Jews and their money had never been returned. Yet the banks still showed little outward sign of regret. In late 1997 the Union Bank of Switzerland finally broke the silence of the banking industry. UBS Director Mathias Cabiallavetta said the bank was sorry 'for errors that had been committed'.[5] Although Cabiallavetta did not elaborate on the errors, for activists working to demonstrate the dark record of Swiss banks during the Holocaust this admission was a step forward.

Despite the carefully constructed words of apology from UBS many observers regarded the arrogance of the Swiss banks as breathtaking. At their worst the bankers seemed incapable of understanding the sensitivities which surrounded the issue of heirless assets.

Like major league politicians top bankers have their own speechwriters, chauffeurs, and personal attendants; they can pick up the phone and get any executive or government official on the line in a matter of minutes. These traits compounded in

Switzerland where a tiny decentralised nation hosts some of the most powerful banks in the world. Swiss bankers, like leading bankers in any country, are not used to answering questions to anyone unless they are very powerful indeed.

Few Jewish activists could summon the sort of financial clout the Swiss banks liked to see in a client, but Edgar Bronfman, the Chairman of the World Jewish Congress (WJC), fitted the bill. Born into the Seagrams distillery empire in Canada, he has successfully diversified the group into a major player in the global leisure and entertainment industry. The Bronfman fortune was built by Edgar's father Sam, who made his money during the prohibition era when Canadian whisky became a highly desired commodity in the dry districts of the United States.

Today the Bronfman family-controlled Seagram empire includes Universal Studios, Tropicana Dole Beverages, the Martell Group, and a minority stake in Time Warner. Overall the group is estimated to be valued at more than US$24 billion and it is still expanding rapidly: in May 1998 it looked set to become the world's biggest recording company after a deal to buy Polygram. And so, when Edgar Bronfman speaks to senior bankers they listen.

Bronfman's top drawer wealth has allowed him to devote most of his time in recent years to philanthropic causes, primarily in his position as Chairman of the World Jewish Congress which he has held since 1981. In the past he has led the WJC to major victories; among his key achievements was his pivotal role in the 1986 exposure of Kurt Waldheim's wartime activities. Waldheim was a former Secretary General of the United Nations who was running for Austrian presidency. The WJC brought to light evidence suggesting that the Austrian politician had been suspected of assisting in war crimes.

Bronfman came late to the Holocaust assets affair. He had treated the issue as just another debate within Jewish life until his now legendary first meeting with Swiss bankers in 1997.

Arriving in Bern for discussions with the SBA on Holocuast assets, 70-year-old Bronfman was hustled into a room where he was not even granted a chair. In a demonstration of diplomatic ineptitude which was shocking even by the standards of Swiss banks, Bronfman and the WJC were offered a deal—the SBA indicated to the WJC delegation that there was US$32 million in secret Swiss accounts relating to the Holocaust era. A set of guidelines for retrieving these funds was suggested by SBA Chairman, George Krayer.

By the time Krayer had finished his statements on secret accounts Bronfman—who at that time had been talking about US$7 billion being unclaimed in Swiss accounts—was ready to explode. Instead of providing a quick settlement the incident provoked Bronfman into kick-starting a major WJC campaign against the banks which is still in progress.

In December 1997 the role of Switzerland during the Nazi era would once again be put on public display when the English Foreign Affairs secretary Robin Cook hosted a major conference on Nazi gold in London attended by representatives of 40 countries.

In the lead-up to the conference the Swiss were not helped by admissions from inside Switzerland that the country's complicity with the Nazis was even wider than many believed. On 1 December, in one of his first public utterances on the issue, the Chairman of the Bergier Commission, Jean-Francois Bergier, said the Swiss commercial banks handled three times more Nazi gold than previously thought.

The new estimate was US$61 million; this was on top of the US$389 million which the Swiss National Bank had bought from the Nazis over the course of the war. Again the Swiss banks were finding the estimated value of Nazi-tainted money which had passed through their vaults was being revised upwards. A total of more than US$400 million in Nazi gold was now being estimated by Switzerland's own commissions; suddenly the billion dollar figures being talked about by Jewish pressure groups no longer seemed outlandish.

Chapter eight

NEW YORK
CONNECTION

Angry and isolated, it was only a matter of time before the Jewish community in Australia would make a concerted effort to act against the Swiss banks. Ernst and Young, the accountants working for the SBA in Sydney, were doing their work in a methodical and efficient fashion, but Australian claimants remained a disparate group in a large country far from the action in New York and Zurich. Moreover, the process was essentially exclusive—it catered for those with the best cases. Who would fight for the majority, the names that were never on any list?

In Washington, D'Amato had puzzled many commentators with his consistent support for US court action against the Swiss banks despite the elaborate mediation procedures which were now available. Few doubted the sincerity of former Federal Reserve Chairman Paul Volcker, the head of the Volcker Commission which was the peak body in the resolution process. But D'Amato believed legal action in the courts was the ultimate weapon against the banks. Only the court system offered the adversarial arena to openly challenge the banks; only the court system provided access to crucial documentation held in the vaults of Zurich and Basel.

As the European-based mediation bureaucracies cranked into gear, lawyers in the United States were mining their own seam through class action activity. The New York-based $20 billion class action led by Edward Fagan received the lion's share of press and media attention. Fagan was a natural publicist, a tough talking New Yorker offering a David and Goliath story in soundbites for the evening news bulletins. Also, Fagan had become an overnight celebrity lawyer after taking on the Meili case.

Fagan was the face on the evening news but D'Amato's office was watching another lawyer just as closely. Michael Hausfield, the prince of US class actions, had been retained by the Simon Wiesenthal Center in Los Angeles. He had an unrivalled track record and the implicit support of the leading bodies of international Jewry.

Hausfield had led the most successful US class action ever seen against the oil multinational Exxon in the late 1980s. The victory for victims of the *Exxon Valdez*, where an oil tanker had poured millions of slick onto the pristine waters of the northern Pacific, was a circuit breaker in US legal history. The case revealed the potential power of the class action process, particularly where there is strong evidence of wrongdoing but a lack of cohesion among individual defendants.

Fresh from winning a US$178 million settlement from Texaco in a race discrimination case, Hausfield might have played second fiddle to Fagan on the evening news but he had access to a network of legal power in the United States which was second to none. Ultimately the two men would cooperate as the key lawyers in the major class action cases against the Swiss banking system.

At this stage in Australia, Henry Burstyner, who had also prompted widespread interest with his settlement for Stephen Baruch against the Swiss Bank Corporation, was the best known lawyer on the issue of Holocaust assets. But as a private lawyer working on his own, Burstyner only retained clients with exceptionally strong cases.

Separately a string of law firms had become involved in representing Australian Jews in restitution cases with East European governments, mostly on property issues. However, at the centre of the action, where hundreds of Holocaust survivors were acting in isolation against the world's richest banks, there was a vacuum. Into this vacuum walked Norman Rosenbaum and the Swiss could not have asked for a tougher opponent.

Rosenbaum, a dynamic orthodox Jew, had come to prominence in Australian legal circles initially as a tax expert. As head of the Intelligence Unit at the Australian Tax Office he had built a fearsome reputation as a man who got his way. His unit had changed the nature of Australian tax investigation from a genteel public service procedure to something which occasionally approached a commando raid. His most daring exploit had been ordering a jet on route to Asia back to Darwin so his team could question a business executive over tax evasion. Rosenbaum's reputation might have remained solely as an exceptional tax lawyer rather than a legal crusader for Jewish causes if his family was not struck by the shocking murder of his younger brother in a New York race riot.

Yankel Rosenbaum was a 29-year-old research academic on a three-year scholarship at Melbourne University when he went to New York for a month in August 1992. Visiting New York's libraries by day, he lodged in the evenings with friends in the Crown Heights district of Brooklyn. Crown Heights is a racial hot spot in the

United States; 20 000 Hasidic Jews live alongside an Afro-American population of about 200 000.

On the evening of 19 August the racial tensions in this district of New York boiled when a car driven by a Jew struck two Afro-American children, killing one and injuring the other. In a tense neighbourhood on a summer's night the incident in itself would have tested the community's ability to co-exist. What happened next would spark a riot.

Six years later there is still confusion over what happened in the immediate aftermath of the crash, but uncertainty over the duties of different ambulance services in the city sparked intense anger within the black community. For the following two days the city would tremble with race riots.

On the night of the crash Yankel Rosenbaum was walking through the Crown Heights district unaware of the tragic events unfolding just a few blocks away. Around 10.35 pm he walked upon a gang of black youths who attacked him and he was stabbed twice—once in the waist and once in the back.

He was taken to the casualty ward at King's County Hospital, Brooklyn, a hospital under intense pressure that night as the impact of the rioting hit its casualty unit.

A later report on the case would state there was 'a failure to document vital signs on the patient for more than an hour'.[1] Yankel Rosenbaum died at approximately 2 am.

His death was heading for the status of a footnote in the story of New York's race riots when his brother Norman arrived in New York later that summer. One of the teenagers involved in the fight, Lemrick Nelson, was acquitted on a murder charge during 1992, and many in the City of New York would have liked the matter to have ended there. But Norman Rosenbaum was not about to give in.

In the weeks following Yankel Rosenbaum's death the story had become a cause célèbre in New York, with editorials published in leading newspapers on the lonely death of the Australian student far from home. Norman Rosenbaum began working furiously to build a new case of violating civil rights against the acquitted Nelson and cultivating powerful friends in New York who could bring justice for his brother. Among those friends was D'Amato.

On the street Rosenbaum began looking for witnesses to the Crown Heights incident. The District Attorney's office had been unable to find even one witness, within a few weeks Rosenbaum had found four. As the weeks passed he found himself living in New York more than Melbourne, returning to Australia to visit his family and attending to his responsibilities including lecturing in business law at Melbourne University. From the New York headquarters of the Jewish Lubavitcher sect, Rosenbaum continued to run his private tax practice in Melbourne.

For the next five years he spent the majority of his time in New York building his contacts and assembling his brother's case. In February 1997 Lemrick Nelson and Charles Price (another youth in the riot) were charged with violating Yankel Rosenbaum's civil rights. Rosenbaum had also taken action against the city and hospital authorities by launching a civil case against former New York Mayor, David Dinkins, and a case against the City of New York. In his case brought by the Rosenbaum family and the residents of Crown Heights the plaintiffs alleged that the city administration had failed to adequately protect them during the rioting that summer's night in New York.

The suit said the response of the city and the New York Police Force was insufficient and it had 'permitted, facilitated and effectively condoned' violence against Jewish people.

More than a year later, in April 1998, a New York court finally settled with the Rosenbaum family. The settlement represented a major victory for Rosenbaum and a startling turnaround from a city administration which had virtually closed the case seven years earlier. The 29 plaintiffs in the suit were awarded a US$1.7 million compensatory payment with another US$250 000 being provided to cover legal costs. Rosenbaum and his family were not party to the suit, only Yankel's estate was involved.

As part of the settlement the Mayor of New York, Rudolph Giullani, publicly apologised to the people of Crown Heights and the Rosenbaum family. At a formal ceremony in New York City Hall Mayor Giullani said, 'This is one of the saddest chapters in the recent history of New York City because of the loss of life involved ... but also because of the inadequate response of the city of New York. I apologise to the citizens of Crown Heights, to the Rosenbaum family and to all of the people who were affected by this.'[2]

For Rosenbaum the greatest achievement was the sentencing of Lemrick Nelson who was given a nineteen and a half year maximum jail term for his role in the Yankel Rosenbaum attack. The settlement assured Rosenbaum permanent folk hero status among New York's Jewish community. Indeed the burly Melburnian had become an honorary New Yorker over the last seven years, and since 1997 had been making the first moves in the second major crusade of his legal career—a battle against the Swiss banks.

In late 1996 and early 1997 as the Swiss banks affair began to receive increasing attention from local and international media, dozens of Australian-based claimants began calling Rosenbaum's office. Some asked him to take their case personally, but the majority simply asked Rosenbaum to pass on their thanks to Alfonse D'Amato for the work he was doing in exposing the real role of Swiss banks in the Nazi era.

Accompanied by a Melbourne Rabbi, Itzachk Riesenberg, Rosenbaum visited New York in May 1997 to work further on his brother's case and to establish from the New York-based advocates what could be done for Swiss bank claimants in Australia. In a five-hour meeting with Senator D'Amato and his legal director Greg Rickman, the pair were given full access to D'Amato's resources and offered top-class advice on how to deal with the Swiss banks.

With Rabbi Riesenberg as Director and Norman Rosenbaum as Secretary they formed the Australian Asia Pacific Jewish Restitution Committee (AAPJRC). Their plan was to match the public relations operations unleashed by the Swiss banks in Australia with public advocacy.

The group immediately established links with key US campaigners in the battle against the Swiss banks. Alliances were forged with Alfonse D'Amato, with Michael Hausfield for the Simon Wiesenthal Center and with the World Jewish Restitution Organisation, through Professor Harry Reicher, a visiting professor at Melbourne University and a full-time professor at the University of Philadelphia.

Almost from the very beginning of the Swiss banks affair the United States, particularly New York, had become the chief offshore point-of-attack against the Swiss banks. As early as October 1996 Gizella Weisshaus had launched her US$20 billion class action from the city. By September 1997 the New York State Banking Department had confirmed the city's status as the headquarters of the campaign activity when it opened the

Holocaust Claims Processing Office, a facility that would become a major resource centre for Jewish claimants all over the world, including Australia.

Rosenbaum said at this time, 'This issue has taken on a universal dimension now, it is seen as a major battle for human rights and it crosses all borders, there has been nothing like it since the fight against apartheid a decade ago.'[3]

Within a very short time it had become obvious to Rosenbaum that Australia would harbour a lot more than conventional actions against the Swiss banks. As the letters began to arrive at the AAPJRC from Holocaust survivors across Australia he realised the group had tapped into a barely chartered reservoir of Holocaust history. The majority of inquiries were from claimants seeking justice from Swiss banks, but dozens of letters also arrived concerning insurance policies and property restitution. Rosenbaum said:

> We said we would consider anything. We wanted to be the control centre for the issue, nobody would be turned away. Private lawyers are doing good work for people with relatively advanced cases but we are looking to help those who more typically do not have the luxury of strong documentation or private funding to pay lawyers fees—we are not here to make a profit, we are here to provide advocacy, this is what Australians need now.[4]

Working through Jewish community groups the AAPJRC quickly established a rapport with Holocaust survivors who had never previously entered the public domain with their cases. As Rosenbaum and Riesenberg sorted through the mounds of letters, documents and photographs which accompanied queries from across Australia it emerged that Holocaust survivors who had experienced 'the toughest wars' invariably had weaker cases than those who had escaped before the Nazi era reached its full fury.

Survivors who were spirited away by friends or families from prewar Europe were most likely to have had the comfort of a relatively well-organised departure. In their suitcases or their greatcoats were the insurance policies and bank account numbers that would later provide a rock of evidence when dealing with some of Europe's richest financial institutions. In contrast, those who stumbled out of concentration camps or hiding places across the continent were least likely to have retained the remnants of their family's prewar possessions.

Among the first cases encountered by Rosenbaum was Hillel Perlmutter, a Polish-born Sydney resident who had lived most of his life without telling his full story to anyone, including members of his own family.

Hillel Perlmutter is sitting outside his shop in Sydney's Imperial Arcade as the Thursday evening crowds stroll through the centre. Hillel is aged 77 and his business has now shrunk to just one shop, which he keeps open largely as an entertainment for his wife Frederica and himself. Back in the 1970s he had a string of shops across New South Wales and a partner in Hong Kong with whom he manufactured clothing for sale in Australia and Europe. With a large house in Bellevue Hill, Hillel is the classic study of a successful immigrant who arrived in Australia with little more than a cardboard suitcase and a lot of dreams.

In semi-retirement he is happy now to watch the younger store owners in the Imperial Arcade pitch for business. In the shop-window displays which dot the retail centre the global brand names of the retailing industry are on show: Nike tracksuits jostle for space with Benetton jumpers, Van Heusen shirts are promoted next to Bally shoes.

For Hillel, who can roll up his sleeve and show his concentration camp number A5607 etched permanently on his forearm, the sight of Bally shoes among the retail icons of the late 1990s has a resonance few of his fellow retailers might immediately comprehend. The giant Bally shoe group of Switzerland is relevant in Hillel's case against the Swiss banks. The case goes back to well before the war in the Polish city of Katowice where his father had a chain of shoe shops selling a range of imported and local shoes; among the most popular brand in Majer Perlmutter's shops was Bally of Switzerland.

Alongside Rolex watches, Mont Blanc pens and Lindt chocolates, the Bally shoe group has proved to be one of the great Swiss brand names of the century. In common with its peer brands in other industries it has traded on the Swiss reputation of quality and perfection. But in recent years, the Bally group has been accused of having bought Jewish-owned German shoe factories at bargain prices during the war.

More importantly the group emerged as the subject of a special intelligence report by US agents shortly after the war. Operation Safe Haven Report No. 12179 details the interception in February 1945 of a letter from a Maurice Bossard in Geneva to his relative, Daura Bossard, in London. Bossard claims that tons of leather had been acquired inside Switzerland during the war. He suggests that Bally must have had 'mountains of raw material stored up abroad, for immediate disposal, in any country, as soon as transport services are available'.[5]

The Bossard allegations that Bally was trading in looted leather eventually reached the US consulate in Bern. Bally's role in the war was further darkened by activities at its Frankfurt factory. The overall impression created by the US documents is that Bally was in the thick of leather trading during the war—it virtually controlled the leather trade in Switzerland. And in common with gold, leather became a prized commodity during the war when fortunes could be make from any tradeable good which substituted hard currency. **111**

The circumstantial evidence piling up against Bally has prompted the company to hire a team of historians to investigate its wartime activity.

As a teenager Hillel lived a comfortable life in the city of Katowice, his family had servants and a chauffeur. The family shoe shop chain offered local and international brands like Bally of Switzerland to the more prosperous residents of the region. The shoe retailing business was just one of several business interests run in Silesia by Hillel's father at the time. Majer Perlmutter was also a substantial landlord in the city of Katowice; Hillel has established that his father owned at least 76 units—'workers' cottage' style buildings mostly used by coal miners in the town.

Majer Perlmutter's sales of Bally shoes allowed him more than a new line of retail turnover—it allowed him access to Switzerland.

In 1939 Hillel was seventeen years old, the second eldest of four brothers. His life in Katowice was affected by the war within hours of the German invasion. As Hillel explains:

```
At first it was not too bad. Nothing much seemed to
happened for the first few months, then suddenly the
```

war hit us. We were told to leave Katowice and all our property and the shops were taken over. There were no arrangements for compensation or anything like that, we were just sent to the city of Sosnoweic and told to stay there.

In Sosnoweic the situation started to deteriorate very rapidly. The Germans were killing people on the streets, people were disappearing all the time. My own brother Srulek was grabbed in the street and he just disappeared into thin air. We knew there was real trouble and my father knew it was impossible to say if we would survive the war.

One night he took my elder brother Jakob and I into his room. He said, 'Kids, if there is ever trouble I'm telling you now that I have money in Switzerland.' He said he had 170 000 pounds sterling in a Swiss bank.

For some reason I can only now remember the amount he mentioned. Within weeks of this incident, my brother Jakob and I were taken by the Germans and sent to a forced labour camp, this was around February 1940.

First we went to Annaberg for about nine months, then we were moved to Othmus. In February 1942 we were transferred to Auschwitz. We didn't know it was a death camp, I can remember going into this huge camp on the train. We were lucky I suppose, my brother and I were healthy and strong and they didn't put us in the gas chambers. They made us work.

We were there until June and then they transferred us to Blechammer, where we found our younger brother Srulek. This was a complete surprise; we had no idea what had happened to him. Blechammer was such a huge camp there seemed to be thousands of men everywhere, and they were from everywhere, there were Britons and Russians and French.

It was a terrible place, we were starving and we were beaten. One day I was beaten badly in the head by a German with his rifle butt. We were working under very hard conditions and on top of that the camp started to be bombed on a regular basis by the Allies. You could set your watch by it, the Americans bombed us at night and the British bombed us in the morning. The worst thing of all was you couldn't really run for cover, because Jews were not allowed to go into the bunkers.

In late 1944 the Russians started to move towards
Germany and the Nazis took thousands of us on a death
march in November, it was a fierce winter. My brothers
and I were on it together, it was freezing, all we had
were those striped pyjama suits and wooden thongs. But
we got some cement bags and we put them on under our
pyjamas to keep us from freezing. If these bags had
been discovered we would have been killed immediately.
We marched for nearly three weeks without food in deep
snow, anyone that could not keep up was shot.

Of the 6000 men who were on the march only a few
hundred of us made it to Gross Rosen. All three of
us—Jakob, Srulek and me—survived that march and
arrived at Buchenwald in a terrible condition. Both
my brothers had frozen feet. My older brother Jakob
was taken to one hospital and my younger brother
Srulek was taken to another hospital, which we found
after the liberation had been a hospital where they
conducted medical experiments on patients. My younger
brother Srulek was murdered there.

At this stage things became even more difficult as
the Germans must have known that the Allies were
nearly upon them, as gunshots were heard as close as
nearby Weimar.

The Germans then sped up their 'final solution' by
systematically surrounding individual barracks in the
middle of the night and marching the prisoners to the
forests and shooting them there. As I had been a
prisoner in the camps for four years at that stage I
understood their killing mentality. So another inmate
and I would hide under the just-emptied barracks where
there was space between the floorboards and the
ground. This is how I survived with hardly any
strength left in me, weighing only 36 kilos in the
final days before we were liberated by the Americans
in April in 1945.

After the war we found out that my parents and my
youngest brother Moniek were taken away, we think they
were taken to Auschwitz after they shut the Sosnoweic
ghetto. But my older brother Jakob survived and so
did I. Sometimes I wonder how we did it.

I never went back to Poland again after the war, I
knew I was not going to find anyone there alive. I
went to Marburg where I enrolled in the university, it

was there I met Frederica in 1945. She had survived
the war in Lvov by being hidden with her mother by a
Polish family. The rest of her family had been killed.

After a short while I left the university to begin a
textile trading business with a partner who was also a
concentration camp survivor. In a few months I made
some money for the first time in my life. It was a
time of opportunity, you know, immediately after the
war, East Germany was very short of supplies.

We got married in Marburg in 1946, and we lived in
Germany for a few more years. But we didn't want to
remain in Germany and raise children there. We decided
to emigrate to Australia and in May 1950 we finally
arrived in Sydney Harbour.[6]

In the early 1950s Hillel began making women's clothing and
selling them in a chain of shops under the Elf label. Over the years
he built a major enterprise which thrived on Australia's demand for
locally made clothing.

On one trip to Switzerland he visited the Union Bank of
Switzerland, where he says the bank officials laughed at his
attempts to retrieve the money held by his father. He began writing
to the Swiss Banks Ombudsman in June 1996 about the account. In
1997 he enlisted the Australian Asia Pacific Jewish Restitution
Committee to help him. Rosenbaum believes this case is one of the
most intriguing stories surrounding a family name which has not
yet appeared on the published lists from the Swiss Bankers
Association.

Hillel has also made three trips to Europe and hired a solicitor to
try to investigate the possibility of regaining his father's properties
in Katowice where the 76 workers units are still inhabited and
managed by the city authorities. To date he has had no success with
either case.

Chapter nine

OLD HABITS DIE HARD

At its most sophisticated the property looting inside the Reich might have involved a major corporation acquiring a Jewish business at a heavily discounted price. At its most basic it could be represented by a slum-dwelling neighbour stealing the clothes left in wardrobes by Jewish families sent to the death camps.

In areas such as southern Poland where the scale of the Holocaust was vast, the opportunity for grabbing Jewish assets was almost limitless. From the industrial centres of Lodz, Krakow and Katowice to the farmlands and forests of rural Poland, neighbouring families squatted on property formerly held by Jewish neighbours and allowed the passage of time to authenticate their rights.

Australian claimants seeking Holocaust-era assets have their roots in almost every country in mainland Europe but it is Poland which has the largest share of current activity. For most Polish-born Holocaust survivors the modern post-Solidarity state of Poland has little relevance. To them Poland is the past, it is the land of childhood, and later the land of death and despair from which they fled. It is a complex relationship at once bitter and sentimental.

Typically the Australian claimants left Poland very shortly after the end of the Second World War and travelled often by way of Israel to Australia. In the kitchens and verandas of Melbourne, Sydney, Perth, Adelaide and the Gold Coast they recall a rich culture in a country which they never expected to leave.

Three millions Jews lived in Poland before the war, by 1945 there were officially less than 10 000 in the whole country. Roughly every second victim of the Holocaust was a Polish Jew. Death, disease and starvation were the early killers of Polish Jews hounded into ghettos by the Nazis. Then came the death camps—Treblinka, Auschwitz and Birkenau.

Few of the claimants have returned to Poland since the end of the war. If they did they would find a country which has changed more in the last eight years than the previous two decades. Poland's steady emergence from the bleakness of communism has been marked by a painful analysis of the past. The new freedom in intellectual life has seen a flood of magazines hit the news-stands in Poland as the people exult in a fearless exploration of every conceivable subject, including anti-Semitism.

Martin Gilbert, in his recent book *The Boys*, records interviews with British-based, Polish-born Holocaust survivors of the endemic anti-Semitism rife in Poland throughout the 1930s. Particularly revealing are the recollections of institutionalised anti-Semitism in the schools and the bullying by Catholic boys of the Jewish minority. Yet for most observers the aspect of Polish anti-Semitism that is most disturbing is the activity which took place after the Holocaust era.

While the rest of the world often indulged world Jewry and particularly Israel in the 1950s and 1960s, Poland was still experiencing fierce outbreaks of anti-Semitism. In 1968 the communist leader Wladyslaw Gomulka addressed the Polish people, and during an unambiguous tirade against Jews in the public service he said: 'We have to get rid of them ... they are not patriotic enough.'

Within months of Gomulka's address Jews were again leaving Poland out of fear of anti-Semitism. Gomulka's campaign against Jews, which came to be known as the 'March shock' and related incidents over recent decades have ensured mistrust between Jews and non-Jews remains in Poland. But change is in the air. Throughout 1998 public debate on Jewish culture was more lively than ever before. A regular feature on Sunday afternoons in Warsaw and other urban centres is the 'speak out' where the notion of Jewishness in modern Poland is vigorously debated.

Under the communists, synagogues had been closed and Jewish schools nationalised. Many of Poland's remaining Jews went underground, rarely if ever proclaiming their Jewishness during the communist era. As Poland becomes liberalised in the post-Cold War era there is new hope that the situation may improve. Konstanty Gebert, a Jewish newspaper editor and activist, is a regular guest at 'speak outs'. Commenting on the Holocaust assets issue inside Poland, Gebert says:

People got used to being robbed here, what is more they got used to not getting it back. Now we are seeing some activity in relation to recovery of bank accounts, insurance and property but people are very careful not to get their hopes up.

People in Australia and elsewhere overseas should be aware that here on the ground in Warsaw there is not much of a lobby for restitution—and set against that is a huge lobby for keeping things just the way they are.[1]

One of the major obstacles for Jewish claimants attempting to retrieve property assets inside Poland is the establishment of land title. Under the communists the very notion of land title virtually disappeared; communist authorities actively sought to destroy title, often building large developments such as housing blocks on several titles. Now the reform of the land titles process is a key factor in Poland's positioning for membership of the European Union. A welcome side effect of this reform is that it will speed up restitution claims. But in the end the Polish Government must have the will to fix the issue. Whether that will actually exists is a matter of fierce debate among Poland's tiny Jewish community.

Andrzej Zozula, the executive director of the Union of Polish Synagogues, believes there is a distinct possibility of real progress. Zozula has been reassured by improving rapport enjoyed by the Jewish community in Poland with the national government. He is convinced that among the current ruling coalition in Poland there is the desire to seek resolution on the issue of Holocaust assets.

The collapse of the Iron Curtain in 1989 would be the dam burst for Jewish property claims in Eastern Europe. Until that time the former communist regime had simply sidestepped claims from the war years. The scale of activity in the capitals of Eastern Europe such as Warsaw and Prague eventually triggered a re-examination of the issue in Western Europe, which resulted in several dramatic discoveries particularly in France.

In the summer of 1995 the new French Government led by Jacques Chirac, which had come to office on an anti-corruption platform, became mired in a corruption controversy that harkened back to the shame of the Vichy regime. The story that triggered the controversy revolved around the privileges accorded to a brother-in-law of Chirac who was living in a rent-controlled apartment owned by the city authorities.

It transpired that the apartment block had been built on a prime city site that had previously belonged to a Jewish antique dealer who had been murdered at Auschwitz. Within weeks the city authorities, led by Mayor Jean Tiberi, were forced to reveal that city-owned apartments throughout Paris—particularly in the Marais—occupied space owned by Jews before the war.

The French experience demonstrated how easily property could be taken over in the years after the war and never returned. In almost every Australian-based Jewish family who fled Europe in the war era there has been some dispossession of property, the question is not whether the property was taken but if such properties are worth trying to retrieve.

Many Jewish families, in Eastern Europe particularly, were poor. Their possessions were meagre and the invasion of the Nazis meant the crushing of a culture rather than the wholesale usurpation of significant material assets. But among the Jewish bourgeois of Europe the story was very different. The Nazis sometimes offered rich Jewish families an option about which poorer families could only dream. If a family's possessions were of sufficient scale and complexity the Nazis found it swifter to negotiate with the family directly for the handover of its enterprises. In most cases these families were offered little in return except a guarantee that they could exit Nazi Europe alive.

Many famous families left Europe in this manner—Baron Louis de Rothschild escaped Vienna in this fashion, as did the Weiss family of Budapest. Another example was Arthur Albers, the Viennese grandfather of Eve Mahlab, today one of Australia's most successful business executives and a board member of Westpac Banking Corporation, one of the country's biggest banks.

In 1943 the Albers family had been plunged into crisis when the Nazis sent Arthur Albers, a successful timber merchant, to Buchenwald. Albers' time at Buchenwald is detailed by Bruno Helig in *Men Crucified*, a memoir partly set in the Buchenwald camp. Albers was allowed out of the camp and managed to travel to New York after signing away his business interests to the Nazis. Later in America he re-established himself in the timber industry and his family, including Mahlab, became successful business people around the world.

In the majority of cases, however, the option of safe passage from the camps in return for hard cash was never granted. Instead the Nazis would evict the owners and acquire the assets. Almost immediately the authorities would then either loot the property, as in the case of Siegmund Siegreich where IG Farben reportedly ransacked his grandfather's factory or more commonly the Nazis installed a *Treuhander* to manage looted assets.

The position of the *Treuhander* was crucial in any business under Nazi control. In some cases the position might be taken by a complete outsider, in other situations it might have been a former employee of the factory who was willing to do the job for the Nazis. Indeed, the behaviour of the *Treuhander* remains important for claimants attempting to retrieve assets from European governments using the evidence of aging *Treuhanders* as the basis for their claims.

In the 1930s family businesses were run on different lines from the way they operate today. Several families were often involved in the ownership and management of an enterprise and families lived on site. Apartments would be built over shops or above warehouses or within the grounds of mills and factories. Once the Nazis took over an enterprise a family's living quarters were also subsumed into the Reich.

It is estimated that more than a thousand Australian families have retrieved or are attempting to retrieve Holocaust-era property assets. However, unlike the claims against Swiss banks or insurance companies there is no central point of reference, and there is no active lobby group. In the vast majority of cases families act by themselves, often spending years in the search for long-lost houses, factories and farms.

The prospect of success is based on variables such as documentation, the later history of the buildings in question and the scale and complexity of the individual claims. But the most important factor appears to be the prevailing attitude towards restitution held by the ruling regime in any given country at a particular time.

Consequently, when assessing Andrzej Zozula's interpretation of the Polish situation, it is important to remember the position of the Jews in Poland today. A minority of about 10 000 people in a land of 38 million, Jews have very little political influence. Unlike most cities in Europe Jews in traditional dress are not to be seen on the streets of Warsaw. And while Zozula's enthusiasm is sincere, he makes his comments during an interview at Warsaw's Jewish community centre which has a security guard at its front gate and a Swastika scrawled on its back wall.

On summer nights when bushfires send black plumes of smoke into the sky, Krystyna Hugon watches appalled from the veranda of her North Sydney home. The sight of smoke in the sky always brings back memories of the night she stood as a six-year-old child in the village of Piastow watching the flames rise above the Warsaw ghetto, while inside the city thousands faced certain death by staging a desperate uprising against the Nazis.

Now in her late fifties, Krystyna is a petite blond-haired woman who shows little sign of her age until she speaks with a voice of someone many years older. If Krystyna was scared that night in April 1944, the fear she felt as the sky lit up over Warsaw was nothing compared to the terror the uprising must have wrought in the Kazorowski family who were hiding her.

Krystyna was the only child of a prominent middle-class Warsaw family whose business interests centred on a tannery. Her father Maurice Schreier and her mother Regina Lejzerowicz had a comfortable existence in the city where the family also owned a group of commercial buildings. One of those buildings is today a Warsaw outlet for the Austrian truck company Steyr. Apart from the family home in the city centre there was also a summer house outside the town of Otwock.

Krystyna's mother was educated in Poland but in her late teenage years she attended a finishing school in Switzerland. In a similar fashion to keeping Swiss bank accounts to preserve their wealth, the Polish bourgeoisie were equally keen to send their daughters to Switzerland to learn the refinement and poise deemed a requisite in polite society.

Poland's Jewish bourgeoisie were decimated with a speed unequalled in Europe when the Nazis invaded on 1 September 1939. Within days the Nazis had ordered all Jewish businesses to display a Star of David. Whenever a Nazi official 'visited' a Jewish community all money in Jewish-owned safes was confiscated. Jewish bank accounts were blocked, restrictions were placed on how much money could be kept in a Jewish home. Jews in the tannery industry like the Lejzerowicz family were banned from pursuing their business.

When the Nazis entered Warsaw on 29 September 1939 the city had almost 400 000 Jews—one in three residents in the city were Jewish. By October 1940 the Nazis had created the Warsaw ghetto. Set originally within an 840 acre site the ghetto would shrink during the course of the war as the Nazis continually moved the walls of the ghetto closer together and deported the Jews in their thousands to the death camps.

More than 60 per cent of people inside the ghetto had no income. The vast majority of homes had no heating, and the average number of persons per room was estimated at thirteen. The ghetto population received an average 180 calories a day per capita against the national average outside the ghetto walls of 634, and the national average for Germans at the same time of 2310.

But statistics can only tell us so much. The world of the ghetto is made measurably clearer by Jan Karski, a Polish underground courier who left this description of the Warsaw ghetto of 1942:

> Everywhere there was hunger, misery, the atrocious stench of decomposing bodies, the pitiful moans of dying children, the desperate cries and gasps of a people struggling for life against impossible odds ... the entire population of the ghetto seemed to be living on the street. There was hardly a square yard of empty space. As we picked our way across the mud and rubble, the shadows of what had once been men or women flitted by us in pursuit of someone or something, their eyes blazing with some insane hunger or greed.

As the Nazi blitzkrieg swept over Poland Maurice Schreier was taken away and killed at Auschwitz. Krystyna, who was born in April 1938, was just two years old when she became separated from her mother in the first months of the occupation. For the next three years she was moved about the ghetto by a series of protectors who were alternatively kind or cruel to her as they fought for their own survival in one of the most dreadful environments ever created by mankind. Krystyna remembers:

> Some people treated me well, some people beat me, I had no idea who my parents were, I suppose at the time in the ghetto I was living like an orphan.
>
> We were always hiding or running from one place to another, it is hard to remember everything, yet some things stand out.
>
> The tannery we owned ended up in the heart of the ghetto and I remember it was operating all the time under a *Treuhander*. We were hiding in a loft somewhere in the tannery, there was a group of us and I could

see people on the street being moved around by the
Nazis. I recognised my aunt among the group, there was
screaming and shouting. Then right in front of us they
lined everyone up and shot them, I saw my aunt shot
dead right in front of me.

My mother somehow kept in touch with the *Treuhander*
in the tannery and he in turn kept track of me wherever
I went. My mother had money and she was able to bribe
people all the time ... this is how I survived.

Sometime in 1943 I was spirited out of the ghetto and
placed with a Catholic family who were so good to me I
can never forget it. They had just one child, Boghdan,
who is still there in Poland, we write to each other,
he treated me like a sister. The family had very little
to live on, I remember weeks when we had nothing but
these dehydrated potatoes from which we used to make
soup. All the time they never told me anything about
who I was or my background, it was the safest thing to
do. They raised me as a Catholic and I became quite
settled in the family and in the ways of the village.[2]

For almost three years Krystyna lived with the Kaczorowski family
who took enormous risk to hide her in their home. Under Nazi laws
if they had been found hiding a Jew, the entire family would have
been executed.

Meanwhile, Krystyna's mother Regina continued to survive day to
day inside the city of Warsaw—but outside the walls of the
ghetto—by staying with an old family friend, a Colonel Padjak and
his wife who were living in Noakowskiego Street. In a courtyard on
the street a group of young people would meet regularly to swap
information about the war and listen to the radio. There Regina met
a man named Michael Majewsky who regularly joined the group.
Majewsky was in fact Israel Markus, another Jew who had also
escaped the ghetto,

Slowly Regina and Michael Majewsky become confidants as she
told him of her daughter Krystyna who was hiding outside the city.
The couple fell in love and supported each other in the ghetto until
the uprising in 1943, which saw the Nazis wreak a terrible revenge
on the city. With storm-troopers running through the city and
evacuations taking place every day the couple knew they must get
out of Warsaw or face certain death.

Caught in a throng of people being herded towards a railway station, Michael and Regina along with the Padjaks were convinced that if they entered the station they would end up on a train to a death camp. As the crowd surged along the streets guards lined the roads at regular intervals. Regina's elite education enabled her to speak German in a cultured accent, which she used to its maximum effect with one of the German guards, pleading with him as a fellow German to let her group break away from the line moving towards the station. The guard did not immediately agree to help, but told Regina to come back later and talk to him again.

The group, now utterly dependent on Regina's masquerade, entered an empty house and hid in the cellar. After some hours they decided to go back to the guard and offer him a bottle of vodka which one of the group had pocketed inside their coat.

As Regina approached the guard, a horse-drawn cart came down the street in the opposite direction to the crowds. The guard took the vodka and ordered the driver to take the group in the direction he was travelling. The driver happened to be travelling east through the village of Zalesie Gorne where the Padjaks had a relative who was a parish priest in the local church.

Once safe in the village the priest did all he could to help the group. Regina and Michael found themselves in some safety but acute discomfort as they tried to live in a single unfurnished room with just a mattress on the floor. In the middle of Zalesie Gorne the Nazis had stationed a Panzer division and the villagers were rounded up daily to work for the German Army. Most days Michael found himself digging trenches which were used to hide tanks from Russian warplanes.

Michael and Regina stayed in Zalesie Gorne until the war ended in 1945. Then they returned to Lodz, Michael's home town. They then discovered Regina's husband and Michael's parents and sister had all been killed in concentration camps. There was only one living relative, Krystyna in Piastow, and it had been five years since Regina had last seen her. Krystyna recalls:

I suppose it was 1946 and I was still living in the
village of Piastow. I often thought about my mother
but in many ways as a little eight-year-old girl I was
oblivious to what was happening around me. I was being
raised as a Catholic child in a country place and that

for me was my world. I loved my 'family' and it seemed like life might go on like that forever. Nevertheless, I began to think about my mother, where she might be, how we might meet in the future, and that sort of thing.

I went to bed one night and dreamt about my mother, I dreamt she was going to come and get me. The next morning I got up early and started to prepare myself. I washed my hair, put on my prettiest clothes. I had a little dog called Rikki I put a little bow on him and told him not to leave the house. I was excited like a child can be, though nothing had actually happened.

Somehow I accidentally opened a door and my dog ran out to the gate barking and there was this woman getting out of a car, I knew it was her.

Krystyna and her mother would become very close in later years but Regina refused to talk about any details of the war years. She would sometimes lament their past life and the world that had disappeared around them. But any questioning from Krystyna about particulars, including family wealth, were quickly dismissed. Regina would not even talk about other members of the family: she never told Krystyna that her father had been killed in Auschwitz.

It must have been very hard for my mother, for both of us I suppose. Things rarely worked out as planned. I was very mixed up and confused and there was no way I was going to leave my 'family' so easily.

My mother and Michael must have been very patient. They had come all the way from Lodz, and they had to devise this elaborate way of dealing with me where we went for little holidays. We'd spend a couple of days in Lodz and then go back to the village. Slowly I guess I started to trust them and in September 1946 my mother said we were going on a big holiday together. That was the last time I saw Poland.

I suppose they [Michael and Regina] were trying to build a new life. The entitlements they had back in Poland, especially Regina's rights to the factory and the properties in Warsaw, were the last thing on their minds. They just wanted to get out of there and start again.

They bought American passports from someone in Lodz
and decided to aim for America. Looking back, you know,
they must have really been so desperate because neither
of them could speak English at the time, I don't know
how they thought they might get away with it.

Anyway, I remember we were walking with a big group
of people who were all displaced persons just like us,
and we were journeying westwards across Poland, all of
us trying to get out of the country. I remember there
was a big tent and it just blew over one night. It was
late autumn, I don't remember snow, but there was
plenty of rain. I remember lining up with other kids
and adults for breakfast outside one of these big
tents.

Somewhere near the Austrian border the group finally caught a train
that was going to Innsbruck. Despite the turmoil which reigned in
the period after liberation all European countries were still rigorously
protecting their borders. Krysytna's group got as far as Aachen in
Germany when their journey came to a sudden halt. A border guard

demanded their passports and it did not take long to realise the
papers were fake. Eight-year-old Krystyna now found herself in jail
with Regina and Michael, who were being held as illegal aliens.

In the jail I was so relieved to have certain comforts
again I thought it was fine. At this time the Germans
were trying hard to deal fairly with us, I think
generally they did everything they could after the
war. After weeks travelling on the roads and trains I
enjoyed a real bed and the food we were getting was
the best I'd ever had.

My mother and I were told we could continue on to
Belgium, but Michael could not leave Germany. Of
course we decided to stay with him, and we all ended
up in a displaced persons camp in Bad Reichenhal.

After a few weeks there they let Michael go and we
drifted towards another big camp for displaced people
at Landsberg outside Munich. We didn't stay inside the
camp, instead we lived in a little village called
Buchloe. It was nice and everyone started to live
something like a normal life. Regina and Michael got
married there so he became my official stepfather at
last.

Michael worked inside Landsberg camp as a factory supervisor making clothes. This was his trade, he had worked in clothes factories in Lodz. During the war in Warsaw he had been put working in one of the Nazi factories reconditioning uniforms from soldiers killed in the war so that younger soldiers could wear the uniforms again.

It was in Buchloe that we decided to leave Europe completely. We had relations in Australia and Canada. In a roundabout way we eventually got in contact with Regina Hohenstein, a cousin of my mother in Sydney, who wrote to us and promised she would sponsor us if we came to Australia.

I was eleven when the ship pulled into Sydney Harbour and I suppose my life was very different to the other girls I was to meet in the city.

The Hohensteins were in the clothes business and they told us to bring out some special tailoring machines to Sydney. So we arrived in 1950 with these special machines and lived with them in Bellevue Hill for a while.

Looking back, Sydney in those early days was like paradise to me: the food, the weather, the freedom. I had only been speaking English a very short time but I got into Sydney Girls High School, which was wonderful for me. Thinking about my childhood I can see it has influenced me in so many ways. The most obvious way is my health, I've had a lot of problems, I've never been able to have children, and I have a thyroid condition which can be a real problem.

All my life I've worked in Sydney, it has been a good city for me, I worked in the big law firms for more than a decade. I was married and living in the suburbs, I had a very busy life, I tried to have a family and there were lots of problems. I never got to law college but I did a conveyancing course and understood a lot about the law. I reached a level of professional achievement which has given me much satisfaction.

I never seriously thought about Poland for many years, it is only in recent years that I began to wonder about what we had there and who has it now. What happened to our properties and our wealth. My mother was a very capable women, she would have been smart enough to use Swiss accounts.

It was when I saw the other stories coming out,
especially Stephen Baruch in Sydney getting his money
back from the Swiss Bank Corporation that I thought
about my mother. She had money all through the war,
that is what kept us all going. Her family were
wealthy and she knew Switzerland well. I have searched
the Swiss banks for any reference to Lejzerowicz, it
is not there but I just know they would have used
those banks.

We have made some progress with the properties.
Boghdan is still in Warsaw, he is working on this all
the time. He has been through the records and
identified three houses and the commercial building in
the city which is now being used as a truck garage.

Boghdan was like a brother to me, he has a child of
his own now [Slawomir Kaczorowski] ... Since I don't
have any children I've said to him, if he can he do
the work and establish the claim with the Polish
Government, he can give the properties to his family.

My mother died here some years ago, but Michael is
still going strong. He is 83 now and lives in Double
Bay. We have tried various ways of seeking
compensation for the war years. We both entered
applications under the claims conference and I was
told I was not entitled to anything. Michael was told
he would get a once-off payment of $4000 and then
monthly amounts after that. We got the once-off
payment, but the monthly payments never arrived.

I find myself thinking now about Poland all the time,
I've never been back, it's more than 50 years now, but
Boghdan is there. So few Jewish people have any
connections in Poland, so many people were killed. I'm
planning to go back, maybe next year we will do it.

Krystyna Hugon continues to work in isolation in her attempts to find justice with the Polish authorities. As Warsaw's post-Cold War economy becomes one of the investment hot-spots in Europe the commercial building Krystyna Hugon has claimed becomes increasingly valuable.

Poland has been making some moves towards creating a restitution process. But for the moment individual claims like that of Krystyna Hugon—even on commercial sites where there are no complications with residential tenants—are almost impossible to develop since there is no claims procedure within the Polish administration. At an international level, however, there are at last signs that Poland is trying to rehabilitate its international reputation in relation to Holocaust assets.

The vilification of Polish authorities by international Jewish activists has been intense since 1996 when D'Amato stunned a Senate Banking Commission hearing with details of Poland's secret treaty with Switzerland in 1949. This treaty saw the Swiss handover money in Jewish-owned dormant accounts to the Polish Government in turn for compensation paid by Communist Poland for assets owned by Swiss citizens that had been held in the country.

In December 1997, just days before the first major international conference on Holocaust assets, the Polish Government moved to restore its reputation with a piece of well-timed diplomacy. It announced details of a plan to return the funds which were taken by the communist government.

Foreign Minister Dariusz Rosati announced that Poland's former communist government had 'improperly used money left in Swiss banks by Poles who died in the war, including Jews killed in the Holocaust'. According to a Polish inter-ministerial committee, the 1949 deal saw Switzerland receive US$40 million in compensation. Rosati said payments were being transferred up until 1960. While as late as 1975 money from the accounts was going into the Polish budget.

Claimants such as Krystyna Hugon still have a long way to go but there is now hope where previously there was no chance of restitution.

Chapter ten

BEATING THE
SYSTEM

Krystyna Hugon's story typifies the problems facing the majority of property claimants in Australia acting on their own against the authorities of a distant country. The generation that arrived in Australia in the immediate aftermath of the Holocaust is now largely in retirement. In many cases the initial reaction of this generation had been to see Australia or North America as a new world where the past could be put far behind. Returning to Poland, Hungary or Germany was not an option for many of these immigrants, and this complete break with the old world engendered a dynamism in many families.

Regularly this dynamism was channelled into business as some families saw the accumulation of wealth as a protection against the uncertainties of life in a new society. The upper ranks of *Business Review Weekly's* 'Australian Rich 200' list is dotted with Jewish millionaires, such as Marc Besen and Henry Roth, who started life in Eastern Europe.

After his childhood in Romania, Besen and his family escaped the war by coming to Australia. Today he owns the Sussan fashion group and a string of related investments which brings his total wealth above A$500 million. Henry Roth, a Lublin Jew who worked originally as a journalist in prewar Poland, arrived in Sydney after the war and quickly built a fortune, first in textiles and later in property. Today he is valued at A$155 million.

Other families, such as the Kaldors, who came to Melbourne in similar circumstances at the same time, recoiled from the accumulation of material wealth. Jakov Kaldor held the same job in the Fairfield hospital laboratory for almost 30 years, possibly associating wealth and position with the troubles he witnessed in Nazi Europe.

Either way, a common theme across the Jewish community has been a belated examination of prewar life in Europe. As families age and become more comfortable in their adopted country, the urgency and detachment which successful emigration requires finally recedes and a considered review of the past can be at last contemplated. This review can be painful and more often than not accompanied by demanding questions from children and grandchildren who have their own problems adjusting to the history of their families. The depth of these problems should not be underestimated. Among the most active Jewish groups in

Melbourne is 'Second Generation', a support group for the children of Holocaust survivors.

After the collapse of the Berlin Wall in 1989 the questions being asked by 'the second generation' became more urgent as restitution promises to Holocaust survivors gathered pace. In a dress rehearsal for what would come eight years later with the the publication of the dormant account list by the Swiss Bankers Association, a frisson of excitement and hope ran through Australia's Jewish community as the Cold War officially closed with the reunification of Germany. When the reunified German Government opened new procedures for the restitution of Holocaust assets one of the first Australian-based families to explore the process was the extended family of Sydney heiress Charmain Donohoe.

Donohoe's story stands out from the broad stream of property claims lodged by Australians due to the magnitude of the land holdings built by her great-grandfather Richard Israel, one of the wealthiest men in prewar Germany. Richard Israel and his wife Bianca owned an enormous swathe of land in central Germany around Berlin. The family sold much of it in the years leading up to the outbreak of the war in 1939. However, it is clear that some of the land was sold at artificially low prices as the Nazis made it increasingly difficult for Jews to own property in the 1930s.

Despite his vast wealth—the family owned two entire villages—Richard Israel died in dreadful circumstances in Theresienstadt camp in 1942.

At the heart of the Israel family's land holdings was the town of Schulzendorf, 40 kilometres south east of Berlin. There the Israel family owned approximately 4000 properties spread across more than 300 hectares. As the city of Berlin has sprawled into the surrounding countryside over the last three decades, property around Schulzendorf has become considerably more valuable. Much of this land has now been rezoned for industrial development.

Separately the family owned an estate in the village of Henningsdorf north of Berlin. Inside Berlin, Israel owned a string of key commercial sites including a retail site on the Fredrichstrasse, one the city's major streets.

Between 1990 and 1992 the Israel family, including Charmain Donohoe, launched a series of claims worth more than A$1 billion on the lost estates of Richard Israel. Since that time the family, like the majority of families who have recovered private property in former Eastern Bloc countries, have remained extremely guarded in revealing any detail of the claim's progress. However, Charmain's husband Richard Donohoe has publicly conceded that more than 440 of around 500 separate claims lodged by the family had been rejected.

Owing to the scale of their claim, the relations of Richard Israel quickly came to the attention of residents and community leaders in the villages at Schulzendorf and Henningsdorf. They complained that they had bought their properties at fair prices from the Israel family and the claims being lodged were unreasonable and inaccurate.

In the formal claim for the properties entered by relations of Charmain Donohoe, the family counter-claimed that Richard Israel disposed of the properties under pressure from the Nazi authorities and at prices considerably lower than would have been achieved in a fair market. The family noted how one building in Schulzendorf was used as a women's labour camp and as a barracks for Nazi troops during the war.

Defending the family in 1994, Richard Donohoe told Michael Gill of the *Australian Financial Review*:

> In cases where people were living there [Schulzendorf and Henningsdorf] and bought in good faith, we're not there to take their houses. We're there to clarify, maybe, where the ownership lies. And that's not our role, it's the role of the government. We lodged claims and over the last two and a half years they have made decisions on areas where they say it doesn't belong to Richard Israel at all. If there is a doubt we say, Well, just let them have it.
>
> We have got, handed back to us, a few of those little blocks that have got little weekenders on them, and blocks that have got nothing on them. We've got back in the order of 20. There's another 90 in the background being decided.[1]

Richard Israel's home, the elegant Schloss Schulzendorf which is located in the heart of the village of Schulzendorf, has also been returned to the family.

While the Donohoe family found that the size of their grandfather's holdings created a problem in itself, the Melbourne-based Castelan family were able to narrow their focus to one magnificent building which still stands near the Postrasse Spreuffer canal in central Berlin.

Within sight of the Kaiser's palace the district around the Spreuffer canal has remained prestigious throughout the convulsions of German history. The communists would later build the Great Hall of the People in the district while today the area is resurfacing again as a quarter of the city which is dotted with cafes and boutiques.

The Castelan's case centred upon powerful piece of evidence—a letter written in appeal to the German authorities at the time the family were being evicted from their property. In 1992 Dr David Castelan joined other members of his extended family across Australia, Israel and the United Kingdom to build a case against Germany's Amt zur Regelung offener Vermogensfragen (Office for the Settlement of Unresolved Property Issues).

Germany has a reputation as the best country in Europe for dealing efficiently with the issue of restitution. However, in the Castelan case the German Government displayed an attention to detail which was so meticulous as to create a remarkable series of obstacles for the family. Moreover, the eventual resolution of the case was in its way an indictment against the settlement office and the way it deals with Jewish claims.

David Castelan's family properties were located in the old Jewish quarter of the city which dated back to the twelfth century. This quarter had been thriving in the lead-up to the Second World War with 115 separate prayer houses and seventeen synagogues which could seat a total of 25 000 people.

As well-to-do residents of the quarter the Castelan family had built their fortune in the clothing industry. The family business had been particularly successful in the First World War as the Castelans made tunics and jackets for the German Army. After the war the family's main business was making workers' clothes for the great factories of Berlin.

The Castelan brothers—Arthur and Jacob (David Castelan's grandfather)—had come to Berlin from Posen, an industrial city in western Poland. The two men and their families lived in the Postrasse complex which combined their living quarters, a number of rented apartments and the garments factory.

When the Nazis launched their Nuremberg Laws in 1935 all Jewish wealth in Germany was threatened; the laws were a web of openly racist rules and regulations which would disenfranchise all Jews living inside Germany.

The Nazi party was always keen to minimise the publicity surrounding mistreatment of Jews, particularly in Germany. Consequently the Castelan family lost their rights to their properties not in a midnight raid but in a public court. The Berlin Amtssgericht (local court) gave judgment on 23 February 1940 which dismissed an application by the Castelan family for the forced sale proceedings to be set aside on the grounds that 'the owners are all Jewish'.

A copy of this decision with its matter-of-fact anti-Semitism codified into Nazi law was retrieved by the Castelan family lawyers Frere Cholmeley in 1994. The impeccable record keeping of the Nazis would form the basis of the Castelan case. As David Castelan explains:

> In our family there was always the issue of the buildings in Berlin, my father's family had fled Berlin for Palestine. Later the family were scattered around the world, some went to England and some came here to Australia, but through my aunt, Irma Selzer, in Israel, our side of the family all kept in touch on this issue. Irma had made regular enquiries over the years though she never got anywhere with the former East German Government.
>
> Then in 1990 we saw the Berlin Wall come down and things were changing in Eastern Europe, we heard that restitution claims were being reopened and I thought it would be a good time to make a serious effort on the buildings at Postrasse Spreuffer. We were also aware that the former West Germany had a stronger reputation in returning Holocaust-era assets. However, all I can say is, I don't know where this reputation comes from. It is so difficult. It is not official German policy to deny Jewish claims, but it can certainly look like that at times.
>
> I got the process started with some others members of my family and we started by doing what we could in Melbourne by contacting a lawyer who had been recommended to us by a Berlin legal firm. This was around 1992 and we were to spend the next four years

working hard on this case, overall we spent around $50 000 on our case in legal and other expenses. Like so many people we had no documentation. We only had memories and memories are no good when the restitution of property is conditional upon proof of dispossession as a result of persecution by the Nazis.

Nevertheless, in our case we had this very strong legal basis for our claim since my grandfather's letter to the city authorities objecting to the Nazi takeover of the buildings was sitting in the city records.

In March 1994 Frere Cholmeley advised us that the Office for the Settlement of Unresolved Property Issues shared the view that the evidence supported our claim. But almost immediately the city authorities shot back that we had no claim at all, they said that we had already exercised our claim on the buildings.

Pretty quickly we were able to prove that we had a legitimate claim over two thirds of the properties that directly related to the 27 family members who were now involved. Then out of the blue the authorities said the properties had been bombed and this meant the claim was pointless.

This really set us back, we had not seen it coming, in fact we had seen none of these hurdles coming and what was most irritating is that they waited until you had cleared one hurdle before they hit you with the next one. We knew at this stage that we were facing a major gamble, for all we knew we were pouring money down a drain.

But we had a terrific young lawyer, Thomas Kexel, who was really exceptional. He was a bit of a sleuth and he went to work in the city architectural archives and eventually he found records of our buildings and there was clear proof the buildings had not been bombed. It was a real breakthrough, he was able to go back to the authorities with this picture which totally undermined their case.

At this stage we were fairly advanced in the claim and I suppose the word was getting around in Berlin that people were making headway in a claim on the Postrasse Spreuffer.

Inside the former East Germany restitution is big business and not everyone can wait for the authorities to make their judgments so there is a fairly active market in buying and selling property claims. It is all legal and above the counter, and like everything else there are people who have become specialists in this business. We started to get approaches on our claim but we had gone so far we thought we were in sight of an official restitution by the German Government.

Well the German Government received our evidence about the architectural records and they came back to us to say they believed that the property had also been mortgaged at the time my family owned it and that this blocked our claim. A mortgage on the property was really bad news, because at that time if it was the case the property was mortgaged during the war you could not get anywhere. But at this particular hurdle we had a bit of luck in that the German Supreme Court gave a major ruling on this issue the same year and it allowed cases like ours not to be affected by mortgage issues. You must remember that all the time we are trying to push this case through the German authorities from the distinctly awkward position of being in Melbourne or Israel. To battle a case like this you really have to be on the ground.

During the case I travelled to Germany and our lawyer also came out to Melbourne. All the time we were spending money on the case with absolutely no guarantee that we would get anything back, even though we were trying to retrieve what was rightfully ours. In late 1994 the German Government really threw us back to square one when they started to question our credentials. This is after dealing with them for years and passing every conceivable hurdle they could come up with, they wanted to re-examine if we were who we said we were ... that was the last straw.

Among the approaches made to us in relation to the claim was this German property developer who was consolidating a site for redevelopment around our buildings. As the restitution claim got closer and closer to being accepted, its value started to increase substantially.

This developer made us an offer on our share of the properties and it was hard to refuse, we got $3 million which was shared in differing portions between 27 of us and that was the end of our claim. For my family it was good but of course it would have better to have gone all the way, but the bureaucracy is completely stacked against you when you face the German authorities.

Some of us needed the money more than others, but for all of us there was a sense of injustice throughout the case which kept us going. I had an elderly uncle in England, outside Birmingham, and he was a bricklayer all his life; he had never had much in the way of material comfort. By the time he got his share of the payment he was 83.

Sadly, he died soon afterwards. The older people tended to get a larger share of the payout the way it worked. But we all worked together on it and I am very glad we were rewarded in the end for our efforts though the payout came from a non-Jewish property developer who was pretty certain he had a better chance than us of pushing the claim over the line with the authorities.[2]

Chapter eleven

A STORY FROM HOLLAND

Eastern Europe and Russia had been the heart of Jewish culture in the years leading up to the Second World War. In broad terms, the Jews of the east were less assimilated than those of Western Europe. Fiercely traditional Jews in the Shtetls of Poland had little in common with the urban Jews in the great trading cities of Holland.

After the war the two groups had one tragic connection—they were both decimated. While an estimated three million Jews were murdered in the Holocaust in Poland the intensity if not the scale of killing in Holland was almost as frightening.

In May 1940, in only five days, the Nazis had completely taken over Holland. Within a short time the country's Jews, including more than 75 000 in Amsterdam, would have their worlds torn apart. In one of the bitter ironies long forgotten from the Nazi era, it was estimated that one in seven Amsterdam Jews at the time of the occupation had been refugees from Nazi Germany and Austria.

Initially Holland had made earnest attempts to counter the raging anti-Semitism that followed the Nazi takeover. The two groups which most strenuously defended the Jews were the communists and the Church. The communists led a general strike in February 1941, but it was brutally suppressed by the authorities. Separately the Dutch Church—in contrast to the Vatican—regularly spoke out against the Nazi policies.

Once the Nazi authorities had transported local Jews to the camps they immediately seized their property. In 1942 alone the contents of 10 000 apartments in Amsterdam were seized by the Nazis and sent to Germany. The Nazis would follow the same procedure when they looted about 25 000 Jewish-owned apartments in Paris.

Many Dutch Jews, including Erica Moen (nee Deen), represented everything the Nazis despised. They were liberal, artistic and held a deep belief in community values. The Deen family was what we might today call 'New Age', certainly in Holland in the 1940s they would have stood out in the crowd. Erica's vegetarian father, Levie, was a furniture designer who had grown tired of city life in Amsterdam and decided to move his young family to the countryside for a better standard of living.

With eight children—Erica was the third eldest—the Deens would have caused quite a stir when they moved to the little village of Loosdrecht in the district of Hilversum in the mid 1930s. There they opened a small furniture factory.

Despite their urbane background in left-leaning circles in Amsterdam, the family quickly gained affection and respect in the village. Levie sat on the village council and the family were quickly engaged in community life.

Jewish families were common in Amsterdam but not in the countryside. In the town of Hilversum Erica found she was the only Jewish child in her primary school. The family adjusted well to their new life but in the late 1930s business at the furniture factory faltered. Despite this upset the family were more committed than ever to Loosdrecht and they took out the lease on a hotel called the Nieuw Brug.

In May 1940 the Nazis invaded Holland. For sixteen-year-old Erica life in the countryside appeared relatively unaffected by events in the cities, but slowly the atmosphere throughout the Netherlands would change first to one of fear and later to one of terror. Erica's first memory of institutionalised anti-Semitism was when the family had to register with the authorities as Jews and have a 'J' symbol on their identity cards.

Later all the family were made to wear the yellow star. One afternoon shortly after Erica's seventeenth birthday a German officer burst into her classroom in Hilversum and shouted, 'All Jews out.' As Erica recalls:

> The time was now 1942 and the restrictions began in earnest. Our bicycles and radios were confiscated, we were forbidden to talk with neighbours and we could not mix with other people. I could not go anywhere so I stayed at home.
>
> My father was a very open and trusting man, he felt that nothing would happen to us since we had done nothing wrong. But I became increasingly afraid.

Erica had been the only one of the family attending secondary school at this time. Her elder sister had left school, her elder brother was studying engineering, one other sister was doing a mothercraft course, while the two youngest children were attending primary school in the village.

Erica filled her days teaching the two children to read and write since they too were banned from school. Then one day Erica's boyfriend David arrived from Hilversum in great haste. His parents had been taken by the Nazis to Westerbork.

Westerbork would feature in the lives of all Dutch Jews during the war; it was the central point of command for the Nazi plan to rid Holland of Jews. More than 100 000 Jews would go through the gates of the camp in the north east corner of the country and would never be seen again. Ironically, Westerbork was originally planned as a site to support Jews fleeing from the rest of Europe who were arriving in Holland. The construction of the camp had actually been financed by the Dutch Government and guaranteed by institutions connected with Dutch Jewry in 1939.

David and his brother had escaped the Nazi round-up by hiding under beds. For the moment the boys were safe but the news sent terror through the Deen family who had just received a string of workcamp notices from the Nazi authorities. At 53 and 50 years of age respectively Levie and Marianne Deen were regarded as too old to be of use to the Reich, but four of their six children were instructed to report to workcamp. Erica was on the list along with her 21-year-old sister Sonja, nineteen-year-old Harrold Deen and sixteen-year old Rebecca Deen.

Within hours of the workcamp notices arriving at the Nieuw Brug Hotel the family began making survival plans with Harrold and Rebecca combing the neighbourhood for a safe hiding place. They found a farm at Haarlemmermeer where a local farmer agreed to hide them. However, a farmhand would eventually tip off the authorities, on 7 July 1943. Nine days later, Harrold and Rebecca were killed at Sobibor, a death camp in central Poland.

Sonja Deen was also in hiding and survived most of the war living with the family of Barend Looyegoed in a secluded farmhouse outside the hamlet of Ermelo. She helped rescue several Allied airmen who landed in the area of Apeldoorn. In one such rescue she was captured and transported to Westerbork where she was put to work recycling batteries.

Sonja was one of the few Jews who entered the gates of Westerbork and managed to survive. In the final months of the war when the camp was in a deplorable condition she lived and worked among the remnants of Holland's Jewish population. By 12 April 1945 when the camp was liberated by the Allies there were only 876 prisoners still in Westerbork, Sonja Deen was one of them.

The experience of Erica and David was different again. They had rushed from Loosdrecht to Hilversum hoping they could hide in the city until the trouble blew over. Like millions of Jews across Europe their innocence now looks tragically naive. But few in Holland fully realised the atrocities the Nazis were committing in Eastern Europe and fewer still would envisage the carnage to come.

On the road to Hilversum the two teenagers ripped off the yellow stars from their coats and made their way to what was meant to be a safe house run by two elderly ladies. But after just one night the two women were overcome by fear and pleaded with David and Erica to leave the house, afraid they too would become targets of the authorities. Almost immediately Erica and David got in touch with the Dutch underground which took them into their care.

At this point David and Erica were taken in different directions by the underground, with Erica travelling to the town of Lemele where she was brought to the house of a church minister.

As Erica recalled in a recent family history compiled by her son Martin Moen:

After a short stay in Lemele the minister took me to Lemelerveld farm in the district and I remained there for almost a year. My hiding place was a little attic in the ceiling. The farm was very isolated and some of the time I was free in the house, for we could see people approaching from quite a long way away.

The farmer [Hendrik Groetemarsink] and his wife [Mina] were a lovely childless couple and we became very fond of each other. When I visited them after the war the farmer said to me, 'I would have liked to adopt you.'

I was given my food in the attic and when anyone came to the house I had to go upstairs and hide. Towards the end of my stay on the farm, another Jewish girl came to stay with us.

I had a feeling that I should have a safer place to hide in case the Nazis came to search the house. The farmer allowed me to make a little hiding place with bales of hay behind a farm shed. It was really uncanny, for the week I made my hiding place the Nazis came.

The other girl escaped on a bicycle, but she was caught and never heard of again. I saw the big truck approaching up the road from the distance with its white hood and I was terrified. I hid in my little shelter of hay while they searched everywhere. They even shot through the hay and missed me.

In searching the house they found a coat the other girl had left behind, with the mark where the Star of David had been sewn. So they took the farmer away and left a message with his wife. I had to give myself up to the Germans before 6 pm the next day in order to have the farmer released.

His wife contacted the minister. She was very afraid and thought I should give myself up. The minister knew that this mean certain death for me and told me to hide in the fields. I can remember it was raining. I was crazed with fear and hid in the fields between the high wheat.

The Germans did not carry out their threat to the farmer and he was allowed home the next day. Of course I could no longer return to the farm, for now it was under surveillance by the Dutch Nazis who worked in close collaboration with the Germans. In the two days I hid in among the wheat in the rain, I was so terrified that even the shapes of the white cows in the fields frightened me. They were connected in my mind with the white hood of the Nazi truck and I was hysterical with fear.

The brother-in-law of the minister who had placed me on the first farm was also a minister and also a member of the resistance. Under cover of darkness I was taken to his home in Apeldoorn and another hiding place was found for me. This time I was hidden in another tiny attic. The house was next door to the church and on three occasions, when house searches took place, I had to be hidden in the vaults below the church. Each time I had to remain there for more than a day and it was a horrible experience. The vaults were only about a metre and a half high and I had to crouch or lie, while the rats crawled around, and sometimes over me. The air was damp and difficult to breathe. Still, I stayed with that family for months until the house searches just became too frequent. In fact soon after I left the Nazis actually searched the vaults and would have found my hiding place when they were looking for valuables.[1]

In the following weeks Erica would continue her odyssey of terror through the villages of Holland, always just one step ahead of the Nazis and their collaborators. Then, disguised as a nurse, she was moved to the village of Sipulco where she stayed until liberation in 1945.

In the immediate aftermath of the liberation there was a prohibition on all travel across the countryside as the authorities tried to monitor the situation. But as Erica recalls she was determined to find out what had happened to her family over the last three years. Risking her life she swam across the River Ussel to avoid the authorities in the local village.

In May 1945, after surviving three years of terror and hiding, and having recently seen off an assault attempt by one of her 'liberators', Erica Deen stumbled into Loosdrecht. She was the first of the family to return to the village and walking to the family hotel she found it open for business and being managed by another family. Utterly penniless and friendless with no trace of her family, she walked as in a daze to the town hall where she asked the municipal authorities for accommodation.

In the coming months the rest of the family would emerge from their hiding places in rural Holland to stage a partial reunification. Sonja had survived Westerbork. Erica's younger brother and sister—Ellen and Louis—had been kept in safe houses. Her father Levie had also survived in a safe house while her mother Marianne had worked as a housekeeper in the home of Jan Van Zutphen, a friend of the family who had been the middleman in linking the family with many of their protectors. Erica met her old boyfriend David again but the teenage relationship did not rekindle. In 1946 she married a pastry cook, Klaas Moen, who had fought with the Dutch resistance movement.

Shortly after the war they emigrated to Australia, with Klaas coming out first and stepping off a Dutch freighter *Mael Suyker* at Fremantle in June 1949. Erica and her son Martin followed on the SS *Volendam* in January 1950.

Martin Moen now lives in Perth and is seeking compensation for the trials and impoverishment forced on his mother's family after they were evicted from their family business, their lease on the Nieuw Brug Hotel in Loosdrecht. He has visited the village of his birth and the site of the family's persecution by the Nazis.

In June 1997 the Dutch Government's Van Kemenade Commission, which is currently examining the role of Holland in relation to Nazi gold, said it would broaden the scope of the examination to include the issue of Holocaust assets. Dutch Jewish pressure groups had been lobbying the Hague for months to increase the power of the Van Kemenade Commission claiming Dutch financial institutions still hold about US$500 million in funds from Jews who died during the war.

Martin Moen says:

> I intend to explore my family's rights under any authority that exists, I was heartened to hear about the Van Kemenade Commission because I don't believe Erica has ever received anything like the sort of tribute she should receive for what she went through.
>
> The hotel is still there to this day and the Dutch are first class when it comes to keeping records, I don't think it should be too hard to prove that Erica's family were thrown out from their family business and terrorised for four years. Her brother and her sister were killed, her father's family were completely wiped out and she went through hell hiding in one house after another, I cannot stand by and not see something like this through.[2]

Chapter twelve

CALLED TO
ACCOUNT

A hot January evening in Melbourne, Norman Rosenbaum and Rabbi Itzachk Riesenberg are sitting in Lamzanis kosher restaurant eating Chinese food. Rosenbaum is just back from yet another trip to New York where he has been preparing for the sentencing by a Brooklyn court of his brother's killers.

In this part of the world January means summer holidays, and friends and family from across the Jewish diaspora regularly make the trip to Australia to get away from colder weather in the Northern Hemisphere. Scattered among the long tables in this brightly lit restaurant are fresh-faced energetic Australians, old heavily accented East Europeans and the occasional brash tones of a New Yorker. One after another, orthodox Jewish families enter the restaurant invariably led by bearded men who have allowed themselves the luxury of taking off their black jackets as a concession to the heat.

Rabbi Riesenberg, who runs one of the city's biggest Jewish schools, Yeshivah College, constantly leaves the table to answer calls on his mobile phone. Meanwhile, Rosenbaum is voluble and expansive discussing international Jewish issues and waving to a seemingly endless string of acquaintances around the restaurant.

The magnitude of the Holocaust assets affair has slowly dawned on these two orthodox Jewish men. A minority within a minority in Australian society, they have found themselves in the middle of an odyssey which has taken them well beyond the confines of their tightly knit community. From a relatively simple plan to form a non-profit support group for claimants taking action against Swiss banks their venture has developed to encompass the widest possible definition of Holocaust assets including property, insurance, art and collectables.

'You know, I still have a private practice, its hard to believe sometimes,' says Rosenbaum.

'This affair has just started to subsume our whole lives, it's incredible, and the cases that are out there around Australia, around the world, they are staggering. Now it's going beyond the banks, and I must say that insurance is the one asset class where I believe there are a huge number of issues which have yet to be addressed.

'In many ways dealing with insurance claims is often much easier than dealing with Swiss bank accounts for the simple reason that insurance policies are not secret. In practical terms a claimant need not be so dependent on documentary evidence. If a claimant came from a certain village at a certain time and the family were in a particular business, providing you have the name of the insurer, the insurance company should be able to identify the insurance policy which is at question through their historical records.

'The next question being what happened to it? Or more precisely … what is the company's policy in relation to situations like this?'[1]

In January 1998, just one month after the historic Nazi gold conference in London, a hearing took place in California which signalled major changes to come in the Holocaust assets affair. With help from the Los Angeles-based Simon Wiesenthal Center the State of California began hearings on the 'The role of Swiss banks and European insurance companies in World War II'.

These hearings were pivotal in the evolution of Holocaust asset restitution procedures because they represented a major extension of government-based investigations into non-bank assets such as life insurance policies which had never been paid out. With the exception of one well-publicised class action out of New York, the great insurance houses of Europe had stood back and watched the Swiss banks take all the heat in the international debate over wartime policies of major financial institutions.

As New York had emerged as the battleground against Swiss banks, the location of the Simon Wiesenthal Center in California coupled with the strong interest in the issue shown by California State Treasurer, Matt Fong, and Insurance Commissioner, Chuck Quackenbush, ensured America's most populous state was quickly becoming the crucible of insurance-related activity.

In an episode similar to Edgar Bronfman's snub by the Swiss Bankers Association which triggered a dramatic response from the World Jewish Congress against Swiss banks, Quackenbush had only begun preliminary investigations into the insurance industry when he became infuriated by the Italian insurer Assicurazioni Generali. Quackenbush's office had subpoenaed the insurer to attend the San Francisco hearings, Assicurazioni Generali had ignored the subpoena.

The insurance hearings in San Francisco reprised the hearings that D'Amato had held in Washington a year earlier with Holocaust survivors taking the stand and testifying, often in emotional language, against the intransigence of major financial institutions. Within weeks California produced the second class action to be filed against European insurers. The families of five Holocaust victims sought US$135 million from Assicurazioni Generali.

The German insurer Allianz would also emerge at the hearings as a major source of disputed claims with Jewish groups. The hearings were told that Allianz had taken almost 2000 requests from Holocaust survivors pertaining to 'lost' policies. Allianz has a particularly dark history among Nazi-era financial institutions: a former Allianz Chief Executive, Kurt Schmitt, had been Hitler's first Minister of the Economy. Separately, a San Francisco legal team attending the hearings—Heller Ehrman White and McAuliffe—said documents existed which would show that Allianz had paid out Jewish-owned policies for property damaged on Kristallnacht, at discounted prices, to officials of the Reich.

In their defence the insurance companies in the dock at the California hearings said they lost policies during the rise of communism as the operations in Central and Eastern Europe were nationalised. To prove their point Assicurazioni General showed how the insurance company had lost possession of almost 150 European buildings after the Second World War.

No doubt many insurers found the situation both during and after the war virtually impossible to deal with since the conventions of the insurance industry did not allow for the upheaval witnessed in Europe during those decades. But the question which burned in the mind of Chuck Quackenbush in January 1998 was, what are the insurers doing about these claims now? After all, Eastern Europe was no longer a communist zone, in fact it was seen as a major 'new' market for insurance companies seeking sources of revenue.

More than any other insurer, Assicurazioni Generali had questions to answer. For eastern European Jews it had been the company of choice in the period leading up to the Second World War. Assicurazioni Generali had always been a strong brand name supported by a wide agent network, and it held the additional attraction that it was not German. As Quackenbush explained: 'We're focusing on Generali because they are believed to have written about 80 per cent of all life and property insurance policies issued to central and east European Holocaust victims.'

Following the California hearings and the coverage surrounding Generali's wartime records, politicians throughout the United States began to digest the scale of the insurance issue in relation to Holocaust assets. Elan Steinberg, a director of the World Jewish Congress, left nobody in any doubt about the breadth of the insurance issue, suggesting the total value of heirless insurance policies is greater than that of so-called Nazi gold.

Certainly the issue within the insurance market was vast and almost completely unexplored. In many cases European insurance companies had literally jettisoned their responsibilities in relation to Jewish policy holders during the Holocaust and in the decades after the war as the communists swept across Eastern Europe.

In the United States House of Representatives on 2 February 1998, two members—Mark Foley, a Florida Republican, and Eliot Engel, a New York Democrat—put forward a brace of bills which aimed to deal with European insurers in North America. Both bills suggested penalising European insurers who did not cooperate with investigations into wartime activity.

One month later, the bête noire of the Swiss banks, Alfonse D'Amato, waded into the affair. With fresh experience of dealing with Swiss banks, D'Amato hit the ground running when he went before the US House of Representatives Banking Commission. He proposed a major international investigation of insurance companies modelled on the Volcker Commission. He also called for the insurance companies at the centre of the debate to finance the investigation. D'Amato wanted the insurers to open their files on wartime policies.

As reports circulated that Assicurazioni Generali had 'discovered' a warehouse with details of more than 300 000 pre-1945 policies as late as October 1997, a string of major European insurance activities which had records dating back to the war years were suddenly looking very exposed. Two Swiss companies, Winterthur and Baloise, issued a statement to the US-based regulatory body, the National Association of Insurance Commissioners, that they did not intend to follow D'Amato's proposals since it would violate Swiss legislation.

The New York senator would return to these issues, but in the meantime he ensured the major Swiss banking and insurance institutions would not forget his attendance at the hearings. After a long discussion on the issues surrounding Holocaust assets D'Amato endorsed a weapon Jewish groups had been considering for more than twelve months—the threat of economic sanctions.

Nothing would hurt Swiss and other European institutions harder than sanctions in the United States. The United States had played this controversial game before in its dealings with South Africa and the apartheid regime in the 1980s. Now an issue of similar scope had come to the political stage and D'Amato knew he had the backing of dozens of politicians and senior bureaucrats in the strategy he was now revealing to the Washington press corps.

Sanctions had already been tested a year earlier when the State of New York had temporarily barred Union Bank of Switzerland from participating in bond raisings. The direct loss of earnings to UBS from this exercise was negligible, but as a means of demonstrating the potential leverage US financial authorities could exercise through sanctions, the measure was highly efficient.

In Australia the AAPJRC, under Norman Rosenbaum, added its voice to D'Amato's suggestion that sanctions could be used against the Swiss on both a private and public basis. The merged Union Bank of Switzerland and Swiss Bank Corporation was one of the biggest overseas financial institutions in Australia with more than A$5 billion in assets in the Australian market.

In late March the Swiss were beginning to bite back at D'Amato's proposals with the threat of counter-measures. The Swiss senator Dick Marty suggested that Switzerland should enact 'concrete retorsion measure' if the US sanctions came to pass. Marty was backed by no less than 37 of the 46 members of the Swiss State Council. 'We will not sit back quietly,' he said.[2]

Then, just as the battle between the Swiss and Jewish pressure groups appeared to be sliding into a mire of threats and counter-threats, WJC president Edgar Bronfman told Reuters news agency on 25 March that the Swiss were close to accepting an agreement for a global settlement. Bronfman suggested that negotiations were well advanced and the deal could be done in a month. He indicated the settlement would be for more than US$1 billion and less than $10 billion. Not quite. Within hours the Swiss Bankers Association said they were unaware of any discussion of a settlement.

Nevertheless, it was clear that some diplomatic initiatives were taking place because the Swiss did not deny a settlement was on the agenda. The prospect of a settlement was now set against the prospect of sanctions being imposed against the Swiss. In short, a game of high stakes political brinksmanship was being played between the two sides, represented in this instance by the World Jewish Congress and the Swiss Bankers Association.

If a settlement were to be reached, it was never going to preclude the potential of indiviudal claimants settling with individual banks. Rather a global settlement would be a gesture from the Swiss to 'settle' their financial dues to the Jewish Holocaust survivor community which had dealt with Swiss financial institutions.

On 26 March 1998 most of the world's daily newspapers carried reports that a settlement on the Swiss banks affair had indeed been reached between Jewish pressure groups and the Swiss banks on heirless assets. The reality was a little less exciting—a broad agreement on the 'structure' of settlement negotiations had been reached between the major Swiss banks and key Jewish groups including the WJC. The structure related only to claims on commercial banks. The Swiss National Bank, insurance companies and the Swiss Government were not party to the agreement.

The Swiss immediately used the news of the agreement as an argument to call for an end to the sanctions' threat. Swiss President Flavio Cotti burst forth and said he was 'irritated' by more American threats on the Holocaust assets issue. Switzerland should not participate in a global settlement; 'taxpayers' money will not be spent in this manner,'[3] Cotti said in a blistering riposte which seriously dented the realistic prospect of a global settlement ever getting off the ground.

The Swiss Federal Council also announced in early April that Switzerland would not participate in the international fund for Holocaust victims which had been previewed at London's Nazi gold conference. The council's position was that existing Swiss funds established by the Swiss Governments and the banks were sufficient. These funds were beginning to make financial distributions among the most needy Holocaust survivors in Eastern Europe.

The Holocaust assets issue had now been bubbling for more than two years and trust between the Swiss and Jewish pressure groups appeared more elusive than ever. Yet progress had been made— Swiss banking procedures had improved, the Swiss would never again treat Holocaust survivors with arrogance and disdain as they had done in the past. And at the negotiating tables on the Bahnhofstrasse lawyers acting for individual clients were getting a better hearing than ever before. There was no doubt the Swiss banks had buckled under pressure and there were signs that restitution was an ongoing process which had been given a tremendous filip from the events of 1997.

In contrast, restitution activity outside the Swiss bank system had been left largely unattended. In an important agreement signed on 9 April 1998, a string of major European insurance companies, including Assicurazioni Generali of Italy, Axa of France, Allianz of Germany and Zurich of Switzerland, signed an agreement with key US states to cooperate on issues relating to the Holocaust assets.

For Jewish pressure groups the time was ripe to open the gates a little wider, to look beyond the Bahnhofstrasse to the insurance companies of Europe where the secrets of the recent past had lain dormant since the war.

Chapter thirteen

THE FINE PRINT

By the late 1930s the great insurance companies of Europe—many established in the eighteenth century—had built multinational networks across Europe. Some of these names remain with us today—Donhau of Austria, Prudential of Great Britain, Allianz of Germany.

For Jewish families in Eastern Europe these Western European life insurance companies offered the prospect of a safe haven for family savings. They were secure, prosperous, reliable and most importantly were foreign owned. When the Nazis swarmed into Warsaw in 1939, the tallest building in the city centre was not the headquarters of a local company but the Polish regional office of Prudential Insurance, the London-based finance house. The building still stands today as the Warszawa Hotel.

For activists working on Holocaust asset restitution the contrast between insurance policies bought on the open market and secret Swiss bank accounts was comprehensive. Families took out insurance policies in their own name, there were few intermediaries apart from the insurance agent who in those days was likely to be a tied agent of the insurance house. The record keeping of European insurance companies was impeccable and since the headquarters of the companies often lay outside the theatres of war their files regularly survived undamaged.

As Rosenbaum and Riesenberg sifted through the Australian-based claims against insurers they saw that the profile of insurance claimants strongly mirrored bank claimants: they were often elderly Holocaust survivors who had never told their story to anyone before. Again, those who had the 'toughest wars' invariably had the weakest evidence. Survivors who had endured the dehumanising effects of the Holocaust emerged in the postwar period with little material evidence of the life they had lived before the Nazi era. As they struggled to cope with a new world order in the postwar decades they had often buried their war memories deep in their subconscious.

Now 50 years later, they were ready to return to a distant and painful period of their lives. Most decided to make their claims not because of material issues but because of moral issues. Contracts had been signed and money handed over to major insurance corporations. That money had never been returned and the corporations were still in business, many of them making profits in the very regions where trust had been betrayed a generation ago.

Among the insurance claims that came to Rosenbaum's attention was that of Arthur Shafir. A retired company director who spent his life in the textile industry, Shafir now lives in relative comfort. His home in Melbourne's exclusive suburb of South Yarra displays a wealth of interest in the arts and culture. The hilltop villa complete with swimming pool and tiered gardens shows little of Shafir's early life story, which is an extraordinary catalogue of survival and deception.

Shafir spent most of the war as a Jew posing as a Catholic Pole in the heart of the Third Reich. Working variously as a mechanic, a gardener and an engineer's assistant, he travelled across Austria and Czechoslovakia where Jews were being killed and deported in vast numbers. All through those years Shafir was alone in his disguise as a Polish worker, he had no true friends or confidants and the prospect of a summary execution in the street or a train to the death camps accompanied his every move.

Now a tanned, fit 75 year old, he has never bothered seeking compensation for the trials he was put through during the war years. He has no need for the modest payments he could easily claim from a string of European agencies. But the recent wave of attention focused on the wartime activities of insurance companies triggered a deep-seated anger in Shafir which prompted him to reopen a case which has been closed for more than half a century.

In contrast to many claimants who were young children when the war broke out, Shafir was almost eighteen and his memories of the Holocaust years are vivid. Like many claimants who have only examined the material dimension of their Holocaust experiences in recent years he tells his story with a disarming freshness.

My family was in the hardware trade in Warsaw. Before the war, we lived in Grzybow which was a part of the city where there were dozens of businesses like ours— it is hard to describe today; things were done differently then. It was a wholesale materials store, everything you could imagine in hardware was sold there especially tools and supplies.

There were people serving behind a counter and the stock was kept on the shelves all round the shop. There were offices out the back and we lived in the rooms upstairs. My father was not a wealthy man, it was a middle-class family and we did well enough, but he had four children to raise so it was demanding.

Within days after the war broke out he was ruined because our shop was bombed and completely destroyed. We had to move out and stay with relations, all six of us stayed in one room.

Then some months afterwards things got worse as we were moved into the ghetto. From the rubble of the shop we salvaged quite a bit of stock, we brought that with us. It was something to trade and as time went on being able to trade that stock kept us alive. We were actually from Warsaw and that helped us too, compared to country people who were just lost in the big city.

It was tough, we were in this very crowded old block, hundreds of people living together. We had very little money, but we had our stocks of drills and planers and that sort of thing which kept us going.

Many of the people inside the ghetto had arrived from the surrounding countryside with nothing more than what they could carry. If you've ever tried to walk any distance with heavy weights you do not get far, they were the people who were really in trouble and they were the first to die.

There was people dying everywhere, people just lying in the street dead and other people dying beside them. Sometimes you would see people just clinging onto bits of newspaper for warmth, Poland in winter is freezing.

But at the time we still had no idea how bad things actually were or how bad they would become. In my family we had this notion that Germans were cultured people we did not see them as brutish; the Russians were the ones who had a reputation for crudity.

Before the war, when he was younger, my father had worked for a German concern in Warsaw and he had a reasonably good impression of Germans. So like many people we did not really believe the war would be so bad, the Germans were not shooting and killing in the street, they were careful not to give too much away, at that stage. They used to say in Yiddish, 'It will only last a minute'. There was this notion that the Allies would come and save us and the German Army would collapse pretty quickly.

When the war broke out I had just finished school. I was very good at languages, I was speaking Polish and we had learnt French very thoroughly in school. Separately my father was teaching me German and some Russian.

My father Natan Shafir was born in 1892, so he was about 47 when the Germans invaded. I remember he had an insurance policy with Prudential Insurance, they were the big insurers in Warsaw, in fact they had a big skyscraper in the centre of the city. I believe its still there.

We were in our flat one night, the flat was so small there was no privacy. If someone visited, we would all just sit around, you could not help listening. Anyway, one afternoon before the curfew started this man came to our house, he was talking to my father and he was a dealer. He offered to buy out the insurance policy, this guy was betting the war would end pretty soon. I suppose so he was fooling himself. But he was pretty serious then and he was talking about buying the policy for US$1000 ... it was all American dollars then. My father said he would not sell, which was unfortunate in hindsight. A thousand dollars before the war was a lot of money, but my father would not sign the papers.

Despite the conditions we were in then, my father and this dealer both trusted this insurance company, they never even considered that things would get so bad that an insurance policy would not be honoured.

Around that time I got a chance to work in a garage outside the ghetto. It was in the old Polski Theatre which the Nazis had converted into a huge garage for all the military vehicles—it was an SS garage. Working in the garage we were given enough food to live on, and there was the additional advantage that we were working outside the ghetto where things were not so severe.

It was the summer of 1942 and I was a young man, and I was in some way useful, so I was surviving. People were dying all round, and people were disappearing all the time.

We used to go through this process—coming back to the ghetto we were showered and deloused in Pawiak prison. Some people did not come out the other end, the SS were always around collecting people. There was rumours all the time and then, of course, Adam Czerniakow[1] committed suicide because he could not keep up the facade about deportations and we really started to worry about what was going happen.

Things were getting very rough and in that same period the rest of my whole family were taken away, I was working in the garage all the time. We would leave the ghetto on a Monday morning and come back maybe on Friday night or Saturday morning. I could see the end was coming closer. They were really difficult days, you were scared all the time, but you develop an attitude, you don't flinch. As long as I was working in the garage I was protected. Then one day I came back to our flat from the garage and everyone in my family was gone. It was like a hurricane had gone through the house, clothes on the floor, bits and pieces of stuff lying around. It was August 18, 1942. I don't know where they went, but Treblinka was just 100 kilometres away.

I was alone and I knew I had to run away somewhere. I was staying with these other workers in a Gestapo building, they had these sleeping rooms we used to stay in. So I had to plan a way out. People used to say to me I looked like a Pole, rather than a Jew, if there is such a thing. My family was very assimilated, and I did not have a Yiddish accent or any thing like that, so I realised I had a chance. In the garage I had a very good job, I was in the storeroom, I had pretty good handwriting and I could do Gothic script which was very helpful.

Compared to other people I was doing alright, but I was hungry all the time. The factory was under German supervision but it was pretty reasonable compared to outside. I remember the foreman, a *Volksdeutch* [Polish-born German], who used to walk around singing this song which was a hit at the time—'Everything goes by and by'—he was alright. You know war was a strange time, not everyone behaves badly.

Anyway I was thinking about how I could get out of Warsaw. I was able to get out of the garage for short periods around lunchtime. One day I ran across a few streets to Mr Bienkowski, he had been a business associate of my father's, he was a non-Jew and I knew he had owed him money. So I asked him for some money, not much, and he was pretty helpful.

Then another lunchtime I sneaked out of the garage again. I used to go to Nowy Swiat. In those days it was like a black market boulevard; you could buy anything there. All you had to do was to stand there and someone would come up to you offering everything from US dollars to special foods that were unavailable at the time. Looking back the garage must have been quite relaxed, for instance, Jews were supposed to be put to death if you were not wearing your armband, but we never wore them in the garage.

A guy came up to me on Nowy Swiat and he simply said, 'What do you want?', and I said, 'I want papers.' It was dangerous, of course, these guys could easily hand you over to the authorities. But who cares, I mean we were all condemned to death anyway. You want to outwit the bastards, at least you don't die on their terms, you die at a time of your own choosing.

We arranged to meet again in a couple of days. I was buying papers for myself and a friend of mine. We got the papers a few days later, they were pretty hopeless papers. My name was supposed to be Walter Jurand, and the paper which was like a statutory declaration, said I was born in 1918 in Legionowo outside Warsaw but that was about all it said ... it was pretty flimsy identification. But we had to make the best of it.

That Friday, just before we were to be marched off back to our quarters from the garage, we decided to run away. We ran down a few levels through the garage and out a side door. We ran like hell to the recruiting bureau where they were taking Polish workers to work in Germany.

Of course once I was inside I realised there was a medical and I was circumcised, at that time only Jews used to get circumcised. What could I do? I went ahead with the procedure in front of a panel of doctors. There was this female doctor, I took my clothes off and she definitely saw it. But she didn't react, not a word, she just let it pass. As I said, not everyone behaves the same in wartime.

I thought I was through with the doctors and then I was waiting a day or two and I developed a skin rash.

I couldn't believe it. I was told I'd have to wait and do another medical.

I remember it was summer and I just walked around the streets, I can't remember how long, maybe a few days. I went back to the recruiting office and did the same thing again. Another medical examination, this time with another male doctor. The same thing happened again, he let me through—it was pure luck.

I was recruited into the labour force and they sent me into Germany to the city of Kassell. I pretended to be a Pole who was a qualified turner. The German despised the Poles, our supervisor would insult us and push us around. As Poles we had to wear a sign on our clothes with a big letter 'P'.

We were working in this Henshell factory where they were making locomotives and tanks. When it was time to eat we used to have coupons for 50 grams of bread, have you ever measured 50 grams of bread? It is so tiny you can't really cut that weight. I used to go directly to a bakery with the coupon, sometimes a woman would give you a decent cut of bread, if they hated Poles they would try and do it by the rules—cut exactly 50 grams.

One day I saw a sign for a gardener, a very senior SS officer had this vegetable plot and he wanted someone to tend it. I applied for the job and they took me on, so at the weekends I was working in this SS officer's garden and there was some food around there too. I remember being invited into his home for dinner one day, they were having rabbit which was a real treat during the war. It was a particularly dangerous thing to do but by that stage I had to live with the danger.

Life went on like this until the middle of 1943 when another Pole started to suspect I was a Jew for some reason. He used to shout over at me, 'I'm going to get you, you're a Jew, I know it.'

I was worried about being denounced so a few weeks later there was a major air raid on Kassell and I decided to take advantage of all the confusion. I decided to get out of the city, I had no real plan but I got on a train to Vienna. I could speak German so at the station I said my house had been bombed and I had to travel, they gave me a docket which was called a 'bomb damage certificate' and pretty quickly we were rolling across Germany on this train.

The Gestapo were all over the train, I could not avoid them, they came up to me and started asking questions. I made up this story about having to go to Vienna, I thought my German was good enough. They listened to me for a while then they walked away up the corridor.

So I was pretty excited when the train pulled into Vienna. I jumped off the train onto the platform, I took about two steps and there was a group of Gestapo officers waiting for me, they had followed me all the way.

Of course they thought I was a Pole on the run, not a Jew. They put me first in a prison called Elizabeta and then I was transferred to this labour camp at Lanzendorf. At Lanzendorf when I arrived I had a really tough interrogation by this woman magistrate. She kept quizzing me, she kept saying are you Jewish? She was just trying it on, I kept up my story about being bombed and finally after about two weeks they let me go, they believed I was a Pole and sent me back to Kassell where I'd come from.

But I never got there because on the journey our train was bombed and I was taken off and sent to another prison, this time the Pankrac prison in Prague, where I was placed in a transit cell. Prisoners were coming and going all the time, all types of prisoners like Jehovas Witnesses and other people who were persecuted by the Nazis, but no Jews. I only saw one other Jewish prisoner the whole time I was there.

Then one day they sent me back to Vienna to another transit centre where the Germans were taking people and putting them to work. I was not there long when these people from Siemens, the electricity company, came in and the picked me to work at Laarsberg. This was April 1944, and the factory was mostly underground. I had no idea what they were making there, I was afraid to ask anyone.

It was pretty relaxed there compared to Germany, for instance the Poles did not have to wear a 'P' sign. I worked there for the rest of the war carrying toolbags around for these German engineers. Then one day the Russians came through and it was all over. I never saw

the Russians behaving badly despite all the stories, I
don't think they were ever as bad as the Germans.

After the war I went back to Poland, but there was
no one there. To me Warsaw was just one big cemetery.
I turned around and decided to go to Paris. I posed as
a French prisoner of war, talking to the French
authorities all along the way. It was still 1945 when
I got to Paris.

I had an uncle in Paris, my father's brother Bernard.
He had emigrated there before the First World War and
had survived the Nazi occupation living outside the
city with false papers at Ville Franche. On my first
day in Paris I went to wait for him outside his house
in the 17th arrondisement and I had one of the most
amazing experiences of my life. I walked up to the
house and there was a woman also waiting there, it was
my sister, Nina. She had survived the war like me,
pretending she was Polish. We had both made our way to
Paris and here we were on the same day. Two years
later we both came to Melbourne.

I got my first job in Australia with Dunlop down in
Port Melbourne, later I started working in the
clothing industry in the Flinders Lane district. A few
years later I started working at Invicta, a textile
company owned by my in-laws. We made all sorts of
textile products, blankets were the main product for a
long time, then later we began making carpets.

'Invicta' became a well-known brand and it was good
for business. In the end I think we had more than 700
people working for us.

Just a few years ago it was sold to Shaw industries.
We don't want for money but this insurance policy is a
point of principle. My father owned that policy, he
was 49 and he had been paying in for years, even in
1942 it was worth US$1000 to a dealer. We are looking
for justice. I'm 76 now and it is hard to summon up
the energy to fight something like this, but these
companies have a duty to settle their responsibilities
from that time. Our life could have been a lot easier
if my father had got the money from that policy when
we were in the ghetto.[2]

Norman Rosenbaum found himself responding to the Shafir case
with mixed emotions. The obvious question, Where is the

documentary evidence? can only be followed with an equally logical question, How could there possibly be any?

After monitoring the flow of non-bank cases for several months, Rosenbaum and Riesenberg flew to New York aiming to re-establish many of the contacts Rosenbaum had made during the years he spent building the prosecution case for the murder of his brother.

Across the United States, and in New York in particular, the campaign to recover Holocaust assets continued to trigger widespread support from politicians and the public alike. On 9 September 1997 the New York State Banking Office had established a Holocaust claims processing office, which was mandated with helping any individual seeking to recover assets from banks or insurance companies.

Rosenbaum moved to build links with this office which delivered a magnanimous gesture by offering its services to Australian claimants. Among those Australians who made use of the New York office was Sarah Goldberger.

Insurance claims in both Australia and the United States centred largely on life insurance. In the 1930s the standard product was based on recurring premiums where a certain amount of money was paid at regular intervals providing a lump sum on maturity. However, life insurance was not the sole form of policy popular in those years. Just like today, prewar insurance companies tailored their products to the societies they served. In our anti-smoking era, for example, someone who smokes a packet of cigarettes a day will receive different treatment from an insurer than a non-smoker.

In the prewar era when women had little opportunity to work or earn an income, a daughter's future was uncertain if she did not get married at a relatively young age. In 1930s Czechoslovakia 'dowry insurance' had been long popular among middle-class families who wished to provide a nest egg for their daughters. It offered a hedged bet against the possibility a daughter might be 'left on the shelf'. If the daughter married the policy was paid out as a dowry. If a marriage never eventuated the policy matured providing a lump sum to support the single woman.

When Sarah Goldberger walked through the imposing headquarters of the Donhau Insurance Company in Vienna in 1972, she looked every inch the type of client an insurance multinational likes to have on its books. But Adelaide-based Goldberger had not come to Vienna to create new business for Donhau, she was there to make the company confront its past.

Donhau had not forgotten Goldberger when she went to the enquiries office. The ever-efficient Austrian insurance clerks were able to retrieve details of her original insurance policy quite quickly. But the insurance group had no intention of settling their debt with this woman from another era—an era when insurance companies ignored or enriched themselves on the paid-up policies of Jewish families who had disappeared from their client base.

Sarah Goldberger was born in the city of Chust in what was then Czechoslovakia. Today Chust is in the Ukraine. It was a relatively prosperous regional city in the 1930s. Among the town's best known Jewish families were the Reichmanns. After emigrating to Toronto the Reichmanns would create Olympic and York Ltd, one of the world's biggest property groups which developed London's Canary Wharf. Her parents were wealthy timber merchants who owned forests and related timber industry assets in the Chust region. But the family had fallen on hard times following the death of Sarah's father, Isaac Lazarovits.

Isaac had contracted tuberculosis during World War I. He had spent many years and a small fortune battling the disease, visiting spas as far away as Italy. When he died in Vienna in 1931, Sarah's mother, Helen, found herself a widow with two boys and two girls. Sarah was nine years old.

Although Sarah's family had been well provided for after her father's death, they were left without a major income earner and suddenly the pennies had to be counted. For Helen the main objective was to look after the family and see them provided for in later life.

When Sarah was about twelve her mother decided to take out a dowry insurance policy for her with Donhau, which was a well-established insurer in the region. She bought the policy from a family friend, a Mr Goldberger, who lived in Chust and whose son Les worked as a bookkeeper in the Lazarovits' family timber company.

Because Sarah was nearly a teenager, the payments were steep; most families paid into dowry policies from the time their daughters were born. Under the specific terms of the Donhau policy Sarah would get a lump sum any time after the age of eighteen if she married, or once she turned 23 if she remained single. The policy would also pay out at any time if her mother died. Sarah recalls:

> I was very aware of this policy, it was a big thing for me, it was my future and my mother found it hard to make payments which had to be sent to Donhau at regular intervals. I was eighteen by the time the war broke out, but even then she kept up the payments.

By March 1944, Chust was fully occupied. Sarah was by then 22 years old and engaged to Emanuel Goldberger, the son of a vineyard owner who lived across the Romanian border in Margitta.

> So when the war broke out in Chust, I was just at the threshold of the policy payout, either way I was going to get my money because I was nearly 23 and I was going to be married, also the policy had been paid up to the maximum.
>
> Of course we were not thinking about insurance policies because there was chaos, and Emanuel and I just wanted to protect ourselves and our family. We decided to buy Christian papers and pretend to the authorities we were Christians. At the same time we also arranged to get married and we had a private ceremony in Emanuel's home. So one day I was married in a Jewish ceremony and the next day I was trying to learn about Christianity, learning prayers and other aspects of the religion.
>
> Orodea was the nearest big city, that was where everything was happening and we decided to go there and try and find out what to do. There was great confusion all over the city and we were trying to keep a low profile all the time.
>
> We rented a room in Orodea and we tried to make plans for getting out of there. My mother was still in Chust and my main priority was to try and get her out of the ghetto. On the street everyone was swapping information and we found out about this senior officer in the secret police who would ferry people out of the ghetto for a price.

We had some money which was all in cash, we had no idea how long it would last. All you could do was take things one day at a time. The officer lived in the city of Satu Mare and though I was only 22 and absolutely terrified approaching this man, I was determined to meet him. I remember I got on a train and went to a safe house which had been arranged for me by people I knew.

Arriving in the village, I walked to this officer's house at night and I remember knocking on the front door and he answered it by himself. I remember thinking, if this goes wrong he could finish my life, but then I could also finish his life ... you get these sort of situations during wartime. Anyway, he said he would make efforts to get my mother out of the ghetto. I remember I paid him with some jewellery I was wearing, it was the only valuable I had.

I think it was the next day that he went off to Chust, but on the way things did not work out as planned. I went back to his house that night and he said that his car had been checked and it was too risky. Then he said he would try again the next day and take another route to the ghetto.

The next day came and he actually got as far as Chust, but when he got to there my mother was gone. It was so close, they had been taken to Auschwitz that morning.

My mother had left a letter for me, and this Christian woman who lived near the ghetto gave it to the officer. He took it, because for him it was proof he had made the trip. I have the letter here in my house, but I can't look at it, it is 50 years ago, I still find it very difficult to talk about this.

Back in Orodea we were just surviving day to day. All the time we were scared, but then a time comes when you just don't care, it doesn't matter, you do whatever you must do.

We heard about this group of Jews who were hiding in a bunker and we got involved in bringing them food. They started telling us about their plans, they had to escape across to Romania and we decided we'd go with them.

Romania was not far away from Orodea and there the regime was not so difficult as Hungary under the

Nazis. [Czechslovakia had ceased to exist in the Second World War, the region had become a part of German-controlled Hungary during this period.] There was anti-Semitism, of course, but you could try and live a normal life. The American Joint Emergency Committee were by this time working in Romania and they organised a rescue operation. But first we had to walk across the this no-man's land overnight for about 15 miles. I will never forget it, we knew if anyone saw us we were dead because the Nazis did not ask any questions, they just shot you dead. But we got across the border on 30 June 1944 and there were people waiting for us and it was all quite well organised. Emanuel and I had to split up as everyone was going to Bucharest, the men travelled by truck and the women went by train. In Bucharest we got together again and we stayed there until November. Emanuel got a job as a clerk working for the rescue committee.

Not long afterwards the Russians came over the country and we were able resume something like a normal life in Emanuel's district of Margitta.

As it turned out, of course, in that part of Romania the end of the war was not the end of the troubles. We were living in Margitta and we liked life out there in the vineyards selling wine. But things were changing and the communist regime was getting more and more oppressive. I remember us talking to Emanuel's brother. He had managed to survive Auschwitz and all he wanted to do was settle down. He was saying if you work hard and mind your own business everything will be alright, but people were disappearing all the time. He was sent to the salt mines at one period.

By that time in 1948 I had my first daughter Heddie and we started to think seriously about getting away from Romania. I was Czech by citizenship so we bought these Czech papers which made us half legal, since only Emanuel was using false identity. But we found out after we had paid for the papers that the documents would only allow you to return to Czechoslovakia. That was no good, so we had to try again and this time we got it right. We found out that the Czech Vice Consul in Bucharest could be bribed, but he did not come cheap. What is more, you had to wait until the Consul was away before you could make your move. Anyway we made contact with this Vice Consul and he agreed to get us real Czech passports which would allow you to travel anywhere you like, but the deal was, we had to pay him the price of a car.

He must have been making quite a bit of money out of this sort of thing, and separately it was dangerous for us of course, but we were pretty tough by then. The worst thing that could happen was that we would get in trouble with the authorities, it was not like a few years earlier with the Nazis when you were risking your life all the time.

We did not have much luck with these new Czech passports, we had only got as far as Vienna when Jann Mazaryk was assassinated and the crisis prompted Czechoslovakia into freezing all Czech diplomatic papers, they recalled all Czech passports. We were caught in a trap. So we bought another set of passports, this was the fourth time in my life I had bought false papers, I was getting very used to it. These were Austrian passports and I remember putting our photographs over the other people's names once again. There were so many obstacles I wonder sometimes how we kept going . . . Through all this period I had a small child, it was extremely difficult but I never looked back. I never look back even now very rarely, this is the first time I have told my story like this.

With the new papers we travelled as far as Paris. But because there was no mention of a child on our papers we had to go ahead without Heddie to Paris. This was so hard . . . to leave without my daughter, I was about 28 at the time and Emanuel was around 37. In Paris we were able to sort out the papers and get Heddie to us in our one-room flat which we rented in this old apartment building. This was 1950 in Paris and it was very interesting for us, we stayed in the 14th arrondissement. But the block was awful, there was about 600 people sharing very few facilities.

I had no training in anything, but I went off and got a job as a skirt fitter. I just talked my way into the job, I really wanted to learn a trade and this was a chance. All the time in Paris we were also thinking about moving out of Europe permanently and going to the new world. The US quota for immigrants was just impossible, we would have been waiting forever; it was Uruguay or Australia. My brother, Les Lazarovits, had gone to Adelaide six months earlier so we decide to aim for there.

Sarah and Emanuel arrived with their daughter in Adelaide in 1950. At that time it was a very quiet and homogenous city where Australians welcomed English and Irish migrants; anyone outside this group was regarded with a mixture of suspicion and curiosity.

Armed with the skills she had learned in Paris, Sarah decided to seek a job as a machinist at Linterns, a ladies clothing factory which up until that time had never hired an Eastern European immigrant.

I'll never forget it, I went into Linterns and there was very little unemployment in those days ... So here was someone who had worked in Paris and would clearly have something to offer. This very pleasant gentleman interviewed me and started to finish up by saying, 'We'll get back to you.'

Well, I was still a young woman then but I knew that if someone said something like that to you there was no chance that they were going to give you the job. So I just said it out straight, 'Are you going to give me the job or not? Give me a chance and I won't let you down.'

Then out of the blue they seemed to change their minds, this was a very English place but they gave me a chance. And of course I worked very hard, and I was keen to learn as much as I could and they let me do that too. But I was a real novelty in the factory, the other staff, the girls, they had never worked with a 'new Australian' before and they were so supportive, I will always be grateful.

I had this manager and she was off from work having a baby. So I decided to make a little outfit for her baby. At home in the evenings I used to work on this little outfit and I think I made a few pieces. Well one evening Emanuel comes home with this friend of his who was in the clothing business, and he sees the clothes and says, 'I could sell those for you.' I said, 'Why don't you try?' This man was a manufacturer's agent and he went around Adelaide and got orders for baby clothes from children's shops.

I was in business. Twenty years later we had a big factory, by 1972 when I visited Donhau in Vienna I had 150 people in our factory making baby clothes.

The insurance policy was always in the back of mind, it was not the money so much as the principle which I was concerned with. My mother had made all these sacrifices during those years when I was a teenager to keep up the payments.

So that day in Vienna these two clerks were efficient in that they took out the policy very smartly but they were quite cynical. I mean they were laughing at us trying to dig up this old policy from the war. One of the managers said it was not their business, they said it was the Bratislava agency and they were all responsible for their own policies. He said we could try and work through Bratislava but it would be a waste of time, the money if we ever got it would be in local currency. As one of the managers said to us, 'It wouldn't pay for your stamps.'

I was quite humiliated when we left the building, we were just made a laughing stock. We let the entire affair lay untouched after that until the stories started coming out in the press last year about action being taken in Europe against the great insurance houses over wartime policies.[3]

Sarah's daughter Judy Golberger, a finance executive in New York, is pursuing the claim through the State of New York's Holocaust Claims Processing Office, while Sarah is also working on it in Australia through the AAPJRC. Her case is one of the strongest non-bank claims to have emerged in Australia. It is outstanding in that Sarah herself is the claimant on the policy; with a 50-year gap since the Holocaust the vast majority of war-era claims are taken by relatives or beneficiaries of claimants.

Separately, Sarah has located Les Goldberger, the son of the Donhau agent who sold her mother the policy in Chust. Les Goldberger is now 91 and living in New Haven, Connecticut. He remembers the case clearly and recalls his father's disappointment at the way Sarah was treated. He has helped with depositions in the case and his evidence may be an important building block against Donhau.

Meanwhile, Donhau remains as intractable and arrogant despite the wave of Holocaust claims shocking Europe. Sarah wrote in English to Donhau in late 1997 detailing her entire story. The Viennese company, which is a multinational and would have staff fluent in many languages, sent a letter back to her in German.

The letter, signed by a Dr Schlutles and a Dr Horweg, denied all claims, including any recollection of the incident in 1972 when Sarah visited the Donhau offices and was shown a copy of her policy. The letter claimed the company had no responsibility for the policy.

Rosenbaum believes the case has enormous potential. It may be the precedent case he has been looking for since he first became involved in working to retrieve Holocaust assets. In a striking parallel with the initial response of Swiss Bank Corporation to Stephen Baruch and Henry Burstyner in 1997, Donhau has been obstinate, distant and churlish in its dealing with the Goldberger family. But, crucially, it has not rejected the claim.

Chapter fourteen

TIME TO COLLECT

Once the Nazis had conquered a new territory, the persecution and deportation of the Jewish community would begin almost immediately. This wholesale sacking of Jewish cultural life offered immense opportunities for the aggrandisement of the victors.

The looting of art and collectables was common among Nazis at every level, from the soldier in the street to the most senior officials flanking Hitler. At the top of the Nazi hierarchy there was intense competition for the spoils of war, and with Europe laid before their feet many Nazis plundered the homes and galleries of Europe for anything that might improve their wealth or polish their social cachet.

The rivalry between Goering and Goebbels is well documented, both men ran competing mini-bureaucracies devoted to pillaging the art of Europe. When a precious art object became 'available' after an invasion, Goering and Goebbels would compete to steal what could be stolen—only Hitler's personal staff could get in their way.

The process of looting could be complex. Often senior Nazis actually purchased the art but at considerably lower prices than they might have achieved in a 'free market'. Later the same artworks might be held in private or exhibited in public. But the common thread was the acquisition of art from Jewish families in stressed circumstances.

The pilfering of Europe's Jewish heritage had begun long before the Nazi blitzkrieg. Inside Germany the government in the 1930s had been steadily enacting race laws which disenfranchised the Jewish population. By the time the Nazis began invading neighbouring countries the bureaucracy behind Nazi art looting was highly developed. In keeping with Nazi tradition, looting like any other activity was a specialised function requiring a specialist unit, in this case the Einsatzstab Reichsleiter Rosenberg (ERR).

The position of the Jews in the art world leading up to the Second World War in Europe was enormously influential. Jewish dynasties such as the Rothschilds held huge art collections, while other families active in the dealing world controlled whole warehouses of art and sculpture. Among the most prominent of these dealers were David David-Weil, Jacques Goudstikker, Paul Rosenberg and Georges Wildenstein. The wealth and influence of these key dealers was extraordinary; at the time Paul Rosenberg left Europe for the North America his collection included seven Bonnards, five Degas, five Monets, 21 Matisses, and 33 works by Picasso.

In France—which today has the largest Jewish population in Europe—it is estimated that one third of all art in private hands was taken by the Nazis. In effect, art was a currency in wartime Europe, and nowhere was this more true than in great merchant cities where the best collections, both private and public, were to be found.

In late 1997 a story came to light in the Netherlands which revealed both the power of prewar Jewish collectors and the sad dilemmas their families face today. Jacques Goudstikker was the prince of art dealers in Amsterdam in the 1930s. At the age of 42 he had amassed an extraordinary collection of more than one thousand paintings including masterworks by Cranach, Goya, Rembrandt and Van Dyke. Goudstikker had been attempting to flee Amsterdam in 1942 when he was killed in a freak accident after falling into the hold of the SS *Bodengraven* as the ship journeyed from Dover to Liverpool.

On hearing of Goudstikker's death, Hermann Goering—forever seeking to extend the vast art collection he had built in his private palace, Carinhall—was quickly on the scene delving through the Goudstikker gallery. Goering was photographed leaving the gallery in June 1942.

In keeping with the custom of feigning a conventional art deal, Goering and his agent Alois Miedl first selected what they desired from the Goudstikker gallery and then went to 'negotiate' a sale with the deceased dealer's elderly mother, Desiree. With three out of four Dutch Jews sent to death camps the 70-year-old woman was in no position to negotiate anything. Goering and Miedl bought the collection between them for 2.5 million guilders.

Now the case has burst on the scene in Holland, much to the embarrassment of the Dutch Government which is standing firm behind the legality of an agreement made in dramatic circumstances between an elderly lady and some of the most powerful officers in the Third Reich. Jacques Goudstikker's daughter-in-law, Connecticut-based Marie Von Staher, is determined to reopen the Goudstikker files. The 53-year-old widow claims hundreds of Goudstikker's painting are still untraced and 117 are held in Dutch museums with no detail of their provenance.

The Dutch Government is blocking Ms Von Staher at every turn, claiming the purchase by Goering of the Goudstikker paintings was legitimate. So Ms Von Saher is taking a case against the Netherlands

Government in the courts. She is claiming compensation and greater recognition of the role of her father-in-law in underpinning Dutch public collections. Separately, Ms Von Staher's lawyers argue that Desiree Goudstikker did not have the legal right to sell her son's paintings to Goering at the time.

The Dutch Deputy Culture Minister, Mr Aad Nuis, insists that Desiree Goudstikker's deal with Herman Goering was good enough for the Dutch Government of 50 years ago and the government of that same country today. But the Goudstikker case is unlikely to go away. The story and others like it have fascinated observers throughout the world, particularly in the United States and Italy, where government officials take a very different line to Mr Nuis.

Since the wider issue of Holocaust art assets and their recovery came to prominence following the publication of Lynn Nicholas' *The Rape of Europa* and Hector Feliciano's *Lost Museum*, New York has emerged as the central point of activity in art restitution. The city's vocal Jewish community and the liberal legal establishment of North America have combined to create a potent mix which has already humbled the Swiss banking industry and looks set to make major inroads on European insurers and other financial institutions with a murky record during the Holocaust era.

In January 1998 the two contrasting styles of feisty New Yorkers and reserved Europeans would collide again in a spectacular fashion when the provenance of two paintings by Egon Schiele came under question. *Portrait of Wally* (1912) and *Dead City 111* (1911) were on loan to New York's Museum of Modern Art (MOMA) from the Leopold Foundation of Vienna. The Leopold Foundation is an Austrian Government-funded body associated with the collector Dr Rudolf Leopold. Since the end of World War II both paintings have been the subject of contested claims, particularly the *Portrait of Wally* which had originally belonged to a Viennese gallery owner Lea Bondi Jarray before being sold to a collector Friedrich Welz.

Henry Bondi, a Princeton University academic, and Lea Bondi Jarray's nephew and heir, had revived the claim when the paintings arrived in New York. Bondi's claims were coupled with those of Rita Reif, a *New York Times* journalist, who is a cousin of the original owner of *Dead City 111*, a German cabaret artist, Fritz Grunenbaum, who died in the Dachau concentration camp.

Krystyna Hugon and Boghdan Kaczorowski outside the village of Piastow during the war. The village is now a suburb of Warsaw. Courtesy Krystyna Hugon

Stephen Baruch, the first Australian to receive an individual settlement from the Swiss banking industry since the affair became an international issue in 1995. Courtesy Stephen Baruch

Jakov and Betty Kaldor at home in Doncaster, Victoria. The Kaldor family's correspondence with Union Bank of Switzerland lasted almost fifty years before they achieved a settlement. Courtesy Jakov Kaldor

Jakov Kaldor (second from right), a Yugoslav boy far from home at boarding school in Glarriseg, Switzerland. Soon the school fees would no longer arrive from Dubrovnik. Courtesy Jakov Kaldor

Barrister Norman Rosenbaum (left) and Rabbi Itzachk Riesenberg (right) who have led the campaign for Holocaust era asset restitution in Australia. Courtesy of *BRW*/John Banagan

Sarah Goldberger in prewar Czechslovakia. At the time her mother was making payments on a dowry insurance policy which has yet to be paid out. Courtesy Sarah Goldberger

Sarah and Emanuel Goldberger with their eldest daughter Heddie. This photo is from a fake passport used by the family to escape communist Romania. Courtesy Sarah Goldberger

Salem and Maria Budzyner of Lodz Poland on a skiing holiday at St Moritz, Switzerland in 1936. Courtesy Stephen Baruch

Majer and Regina Perlmutter. Majer's extensive business interests led him regularly to Switzerland where Bally shoes was a client. Courtesy Hillel Perlmutter

Erica Moen (extreme right) with Klaas Moen and Lou Deen in Western Australia. Courtesy Martin Moen

Arthur Shafir at home in Melbourne: 'Our lives could have been a lot easier if my father had got the money from that policy when we were in the ghetto'. Courtesy Arthur Shafir

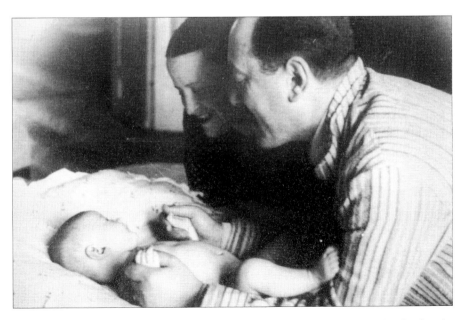

Erica Turek (infant) with Siegmund and Necha Turek. Within months the family would be torn apart with Siegmund dying of typhoid in a Russian labour camp. Courtesy Erica Turek

Siegmund Siegreich (centre) aged 11 in prewar Katowice, Poland with his mother
Eva and sister Helena

The exhibition 'Egon Schiele: The Leopold Collection' was just days away from finishing its run at MOMA when the Bondi and Reif families moved to highlight their claims against the paintings. In the final week of the exhibition the *New York Times* ran an article detailing the controversy behind the two paintings. The families then asked MOMA not to ship the paintings back to Austria. But the gallery explained it was bound by contractual obligations, which are standard under such arrangements, and immediately declined the request.

Under US legislation the owner of an object or a work of art which is stolen retains the ownership after the robbery has been committed. In contrast, under European law, the onus is on the current owner of an object of disputed provenance to prove only that they acquired the object 'in good faith'.

Bearing in mind these legal differences the Leopold Foundation told the contesting families it was prepared to be bound by an international tribunal in the event of an investigation. However, the foundation insisted upon repossessing the paintings first. At this junction in stepped the New York District Attorney Robert Morgenthau, who launched a criminal investigation into the provenance of the two Schiele paintings. Morgenthau effectively confiscated the paintings from their current owners by issuing subpoenas which prevented the works from leaving New York until his investigation was complete.

It was a highly provocative move, unprecedented in the history of international gallery transactions, and one which triggered a new round of activity in relation to art recovery. While both the Bondi and Reif cases are intriguing it was the Bondi case that had triggered Morgenthau's audacious move.

According to Henry Bondi *Portrait of Wally* had hung in the private home of Lea Bondi Jarray in Vienna; the gallery owner had been an early enthusiast of the painter and the first to put his works on show. The Bondi family claim Lea Bondi Jarray was coerced into handing over the painting to the Nazi sympathiser-collector Friedrich Welz shortly after the Nazis entered Austria in 1938. Rudolf Leopold, now 72, has always disputed the Bondi family version of events claiming that Welz had bought the picture in a legitimate transaction. After fleeing Vienna for the United States, Lea Bondi Jarray claimed she had been forced to hand over the *Portrait of Wally* to Welz.

Rudolf Leopold acquired the painting in 1954 from the Austrian Belvedere gallery, which had bought it in 1950 from a Robert Rieger. Leopold's key defence in relation to the painting is that he was assured of its origin by the state-sponsored Austrian gallery in 1954.

Robert Morgenthau wished to check this story for himself, and to do so he had to act fast before the painting returned to Austria. The Austrian Government was shocked at Morgenthau's move, as were many leading figures in the art world. Glenn Lowry, the director of MOMA, said, 'We borrowed these pictures in absolute good faith from an institution which we thought was a good-faith acquirer … what is the moral position for us to say we are going to hold your art?'

The Austrian Culture Minister, Ms Elizabeth Gehrer, said the Morgenthau manoeuvre, 'Dealt a heavy blow to the international exchange of art.'

Morgenthau's chief investigator, Daniel Castleman, responded with typical New York abrasiveness telling the *New York Times* shortly afterwards: 'Why would anyone be surprised that we are investigating stolen property in our jurisdiction?'

Public galleries around the world watched the Egon Schiele affair with trepidation. Regardless of the outcome in the courts, the ability of one city administration to impound works of art which entered its jurisdiction set a very dangerous precedent—it diluted any assurance a gallery could offer a lender that a painting would be secure while on loan from a permanent collection. It was inevitable that copycat incidents would occur in the art world, and within a matter of months the Egon Schiele incident was echoed by events in the unlikely location of Dunedin, New Zealand.

In April 1998 the Dunedin Public Art Gallery emerged at the centre of an international controversy which reached back to World War II and the little-known transfer of a key Italian art collection. The crisis turned on a deal completed in 1994 between the gallery and a local family which allowed Dunedin—a city of 20 000 people in New Zealand's South Island—to acquire a collection that would be the envy of its peers in Auckland and Australia.

The gallery had acquired five paintings from the Macchiaioli school, a highly regarded nineteenth-century school of Italian impressionism. The Dunedin Public Art Gallery Society had paid just NZ$20 000 for the five works. Mr Peter Entwisle, the curator of the gallery at the time, described the deal as the most important historical find in New Zealand for 30 years.

The London-based *Art Newspaper* first reported the provenance of the paintings. It turned out the five works had been in the possession of the Fraser family of Dunedin for the previous 50 years. During the Second World War Dunedin man, Mr Fraser, who had been an amateur painter and art collector, was stationed in a field hospital in central Italy. One afternoon when visiting a souvenir shop he noticed the five paintings and recognised them as works from the Macchiaioli school. Fraser had sent the paintings back to New Zealand and they had remained with his family until his death.

In September 1997, after exhibiting the pictures locally for three years the Dunedin Public Art Gallery received a request from the Pananti Gallery in Florence to borrow the Macchiaioli works for an exhibition. Rarely asked to send paintings to Europe, let alone Florence, the gallery was happy to oblige.

The Dunedin Gallery has not seen the paintings again. Since the end of the Second World War the family of Cino Vitta, a leading figure in the Jewish community in Florence, has been seeking to recover Macchiaioli works which were looted from their father's collection.

When Jonathan and Nathaniel Vitta—Cino Vitta's brothers— heard that Macchiaioli works from New Zealand were on show at the Pananti they immediately took out civil and penal restraints on the works, calling for an investigation into their provenance.

An embittered John McCormick, the director of the Dunedin Gallery at the time of the purchase, defended his gallery and his decision to buy the painting: 'We advised a number of people including people in Italy that the works had turned up and when the request came through to include them in an exhibition we were delighted to accede to that.'[1]

The Macchiaioli paintings are still held in bond in Italy and the Dunedin Gallery may have lost one its greatest claims to fame. The circumstances of the Dunedin paintings are entirely separate to the Leopold collection and there is no recorded history of disputed ownership. But the fact is that the paintings were on the Italian Ministry of Culture's Silverio Catalogue which lists art looted during the Second World War. More than anything else the

Macchiaioli affair demonstrates the continuing fallibility of provenance records in all public galleries despite the on-line data which most gallery curators can now access through the internet.

If the Dunedin Art Gallery, in provincial New Zealand, held works from the Nazi era of debatable provenance then how pure were the great collections of Sydney, Melbourne and the National Gallery of Australia in Canberra, not to mention the private collections of the major Australian corporations and Australia's wealthiest families?

Rosenbaum and Riesenberg at the AAPJRC were not going to wait to find out. In May 1998 they launched a database of assets of Holocaust survivors 'who had artworks, sculptures, collectibles or significant period furniture looted by the Nazis'.[2] The AAPJRC liaised with the United States Holocaust Museum in Washington in designing and servicing the facility. While acting as an advocate for Holocaust survivors the AAPJRC also offered its services to historians, museums and gallery curators wishing to purchase artworks where provenance may be an issue.

The move by Rosenbaum and Riesenberg was welcomed by Jewish families across Australia, but it was too late for Kurt Lippmann and his family. Unlike many Jewish families who are only now seriously examining their claims to artworks from wartime Europe, the Lippmann's know the story of their collection all too well.

One morning late in June 1943 a one-page letter from Germany dropped through Franz Lippmann's letterbox in Melbourne. He looked at the stamp of the International Red Cross on the envelope and knew immediately the letter was from his brother in Hamburg.

The letter, which is still in the possession of the Lippmann family, read: 'in this hour of parting we remember gratefully you and your children's constant love. May the future bring you all happy and wonderful lives. Most sincerely. Leo Israel Lippmann.' A few weeks earlier Leo and his wife Anna had sat together for the last time and shared a vial of poison which killed them both before the Nazis could take them to Theresienstadt.

Even by the standards of Germany in 1943 Leo Lippmann's story was extraordinary. He was an exceptionally able man who had been a city administrator of the first rank. At the age of 36 he had ascended to the office of Secretary of the Senate in Hamburg, effectively the finance manager for one of the greatest ports in the world. Born in 1881 Lippmann had been a leading member of Hamburg's flourishing Jewish community which had been established in the north German city in the seventeenth century.

After taking a law degree Lippmann had entered the city administration and quickly rose through a succession of key posts. As an administrator he had excelled during the First World War when he was responsible for the provision and regulation of food supplies for the city and state of Hamburg. He had attained one of the highest public service positions ever reached by a Jew inside Germany, and his financial expertise had been held in respect in both Jewish and non-Jewish professional circles across the city.

But by the time he wrote the letter to his brother Franz, the master administrator of more than three decades experience had been worn down by the machinations of Nazi Germany. At the time of writing the letter Lippmann was one of the last Jews left in Hamburg. He had watched over the preceding decade as the Nazis took everything away from him and his community. Slowly Jews had been removed from all civic and cultural life in the city. The election of Hitler as Chancellor in 1933 had spelled the end of normal life for Jews across Germany, including Leo Lippmann who had been removed from his post in the city administration shortly after the Nazis came to power.

He would spend the next ten years as an advocate for the steadily shrinking Jewish community in his city, ultimately becoming the President of the Jewish community in Hamburg. As his Melbourne-based nephew Kurt Lippmann explains, 'It was Leo's tragic fate to be president at a time of the decimation and liquidation of that once flourishing community.'[3]

Lippmann was a sophisticated public service mandarin ejected from his position by the hatred and racial prejudice which steadily gripped Hamburg during the Third Reich. By 1941 the deportations from Hamburg to concentration camps—mostly to Theresienstadt —began their dismal traffic. Between 1 January 1941 and 31 December 1942 the number of Jews in the city fell by more than half.

As the deportations continued Lippmann's greatest contribution could only be to help his fellow Jews bear the pressures of the time. He would always go down to the Hamburg railway station to carry out the heartbreaking task of assisting other Jews who were preparing for deportation from the city. As the months passed Lippmann watched as the great city he once managed became a Nazi stronghold. The Jewish population was huddled together in impoverished circumstances within a few city blocks.

Even Jews in mixed marriages were now being targeted as the anti-Semitism of the Nazi administration moved towards the horrific era of 'The Final Solution'. Lippmann's work as President of the Jewish community allowed him to form strong bonds with fellow community leaders including Rabbi Leo Baeck, the theologian and one of the most prominent religious leaders in the Holocaust era. Lippmann also made recordings of the destruction of his community in an important historical monograph which survives to this day—*The Jewish community in Hamburg in the year 1942: The liquidation of Jewish institutions and organisation in Hamburg.*

In the objective language of a public service manager, the document records in passionless detail the destruction of Hamburg's Jewish culture. This detachment from the material facts before him can have the paradoxical effect of making the Lippmann document an indictment of the events he describes. A description of Jewish identification conventions seethes with untold disgust at the pettiness of the Nazi regime where even former soldiers who have been decorated by the country are victimised.

> At the end of 1942 an order was given to prepare a full analysis of the 2409 [Jews] then obliged to wear the Jewish star. The analysis was to be made as at 22nd May 1942. The star had to be worn by all Jews over the age of 6 years, unless special exemption was granted in accordance with paragraph 3 of the police order dated 1st September 1941. The analysis showed, that the total of 2409 Jews consisted of 776 males and 1633 females. Of these 136 males and 222 females could no longer live independently. Included also were 30 men, who had been awarded the war invalids badge or the Iron Cross 1st class.[4]

By the middle of 1942 all Jews in the city were living under an aggressive and unforgiving regime: the front door of Lippmann's house was marked as a Jewish residence. He could no longer buy books or newspapers. He could not use a public telephone or use the waiting room in a railway station. Then on 10 June 1943 the last vestige of normal life for Lippmann was terminated when the Gestapo came and shut down the offices of the Hamburg Jewish Community. Later that day Leo and Anna Lippmann were informed that they were to be deported to Theresienstadt. The last of the remaining Jews in the city led by Rabbi Carlebach had already boarded a train to the concentration camps. By midnight Lippmann had escaped the world he had watched decline into squalor in less than a decade.

Leo Lippmann's last letter to Australia had been to Franz Lippmann, a co-founder of the B'nai B'rith—the Jewish community services group. Over the decades since Franz Lippmann's arrival (he died in 1953) his extended family have produced a string of academics and writers in Melbourne, including Dr Helen Light, the director of the Jewish Museum in St Kilda, who is the daughter of Kurt Lippmann, Franz's son.

Kurt Lippmann and Helen Light were among a group of family members taking a holiday in Europe in 1994 when they went to visit the Hamburg Kunsthalle. There the story of Leo Lippmann resurfaced before them in the form of a long-forgotten coin collection.

Strolling between the exhibition halls in the gallery Helen, who has a doctorate in classics, came upon an impressive collection of Roman coins displayed together under the intriguing title of 'The Lippmann Collection'.

'We knew straightaway that it was my uncle Leo's coin collection and it had got to the gallery in a roundabout way which began when the Nazis stole the collection from him in the 1930s,' Kurt said.[5]

Along with exercising enormous influence over the financial affairs of the city of Hamburg, Leo Lippmann had also been an avid collector of coins from the ancient world. In the Lippmann home in Melbourne a picture exists of Leo Lippmann with a shaved head and a double-breasted suit studying his coin collection. In the sepia-toned photograph Lippmann is the very image of a Weimar Republic financial officer. Then in his thirties Lippmann had built up a collection of coins which spanned from the Roman Republic in the third century BC until the fourth century AD.

The collection mounted by the Hamburg gallery was the remnants of Lippmann's original collection, which had been taken from him by officers of the German Central Bank, the Reichsbank, in 1939. The Reichsbank then used Lippmann's coins, which had taken a lifetime to collect, to inaugurate its own collection of coins from the ancient world.

Keen to establish the full facts surrounding the collection Kurt and Helen sought out an old friend of the family, Hans Christian Albrecht, who was a well-known solicitor in Hamburg. Flanked by his museum curator daughter, Helen Light, and his solicitor Hans Albrecht, Kurt Lippmann returned to the Hamburg Kunsthalle to investigate the full story behind his uncle's prized coin collection.

In an interview with the director of the Hamburg Kunsthalle, Dr George Syamkem, the family discovered that Leo had 'sold' the coins to the Reichsbank in stressed circumstances for 4000 reichsmarks. It was also revealed that after the war members of the Lippmann family had received another 4000 marks in compensation for the events surrounding the removal of the collection.

'We didn't know all this, but having heard it we decided we wouldn't bother claiming for any compensation or anything like that,' says Kurt.

'However, we did believe that as part of the restitution process the role of my uncle in building a collection which was being presented to the people of Hamburg should be fully recorded for all to see.'

With the cooperation of the gallery authorities there is now a plaque above the Lippmann coin collection which describes the circumstance through which the collection was acquired. As the plaque suggests:

Quite apart from its beauty and from the systematic way of its design, the collection of Roman coins displayed illustrates the personality of a man who was a leading personality in this city.

These coins are both silent and eloquent witnesses of an epoch of Hellenistic culture and of human rights which lasted until it collapsed at the end of the Volkerwanderung. This period serves until this day as a model of open and correct administration. It was this then that must have had such as great appeal to this Jewish man, who thirsted for

Justice, to this Jurist who was also an historian and to this expert in finance, who had proved himself in many cases.

The visitor standing before this showcase admiring these coins may well contemplate and reflect on this.

The Lippmann case is over, but the campaigns by the Vitta family in Florence and the Bondi family in New York are far from settled. The issue of Holocaust-era art assets is now emerging as a distinct sphere of activity commensurate in its scope with the hunt for dormant accounts, wartime insurance policies or properties under claim in the former Eastern Bloc.

Nowhere is this more evident than in the salons of New York and Paris where the descendants of Georges Wildenstein, one of Europe's greatest art dealers in the war era, are now defending claims the family has profited from Nazi plunder for three generations.

As one of America's most reported divorce cases the separation battles of Alec—grandson of Georges—and Jocelyne Wildenstein hardly needed further material to fan the interest of the media. But claims the Wildensteins, a Jewish family who still dominate the international art market, traded profitably with the Nazis for several years added spice to the story.

Forty years ago the Wildensteins had been subject to international attention when they were found to be holding a set of fifteenth century enamels belonging to Poland's Czartoryski family before the war. The Wildensteins had settled the issue with the Czartoryski family, but the suspicion that the billionaire Wildensteins profited from Nazi looting has been brewing since that time.

In September 1997 the *New York Times* published a fresh set of allegations connecting the Wildenstein family with looted art works. The story largely concerned the circumstances in which the family had acquired a set of rare medieval manuscripts. An examination of the manuscripts by a Princeton University art historian, James Marrow, revealed markings on the manuscripts which indicated the papers had once belonged to the Kann family, another well-known Jewish family of art dealers at the time of the Second World War.

The Wildensteins strongly denied any suggestion they had dealt with the Nazis but the affair put another question mark over the integrity of one of the world's great dealing houses. It also offered more publicity on the issue of art assets from the Holocaust era than any other event. Indeed the Wildenstein affair emerged just as it seemed the momentum of the battle to return more basic assets belonging to less glamorous people was beginning to fade. A new phase of activity surrounding the recovery of art and collectables may yet herald some of the most important stories still to emerge from the Holocaust era.

Chapter fifteen

WHERE TO NOW?

By late May 1998 the prospect of a global agreement between the major Swiss commerical banks and the peak Jewish pressure groups was back on the table. The US Undersecretary of State Stuart Eizenstat was again ready to step in as mediator. On 27 April, Eizenstat had hosted a major meeting of all parties in Washington, including representatives from the Swiss commerial banks, the lawyers representing the class actions and leading members of Jewish pressure groups such as the World Jewish Congress.

After taking relations between Switzerland and Jewish groups to the brink of open confrontation, the WJC moved to make peace in early May. It was not a moment too soon as the WJC had allowed its aggression to dominate Swiss–Jewish relations in the preceding months. The isolation of the WJC's stance had become all too clear when the highly respected Nazi hunter Simon Wiesenthal had blasted the group's overtly aggressive position a month earlier.

On 12 May, addressing the Swiss Parliament, WJC Secretary Israel Singer made amends to the Swiss people and to Wiesenthal by apologising for a string of harsh words uttered by his Chairman Edgar Bronfman in the preceding months.

By mid May there was a distinct air of détente between the major advocates on both sides of the affair as all parties prepared for the release of the Swiss Government santioned 'Bergier Commission Report'. Chaired by eminent historian Jean-Francois Bergier the 280 page report was a major attempt by the Swiss Government to open the files on Switzerland's role in World War II. A total of 35 historians had toiled for more than two years to produce the document, which was released on 25 May.

For the first time, over and above the thousands of words written in books and newspapers and spoken at a hundred different seminars around the world, the historical facts of Swiss neutrality were laid bare by the panel of experts whose authority was impeccable. Its findings are worth spelling out.

The report said the Swiss National Bank knew that gold sent to Switzerland included looted gold and it confirmed suspicions that some of the gold included gold from Holocaust victims.

According to the report, said the Swiss National Bank had purchased gold worth US$2.5 billion in today's values.

Crucially, it indicated that 119.5 kilograms of victim gold or non-monetary gold was sent to Swiss banks. This was non-bullion gold prepared from the assets of Holocaust victims, such as ornaments and jewellery.

However the report made it clear that officals at the SNB could not have known this gold belonged to Holocaust victims because it had been melted down.

The report detailed specifically how gold belonging to Holocaust victims could end up in Swiss banks through the 'Melmer system' based on the activities of SS Captain Bruno Melmer who was in charge of collecting gold in Auschwitz and Birkenau. The report indicated that some of the gold collected by Melmer was melted down and sent to the Reichsbank account at the Swiss National Bank in Bern.

The report also clearly showed that Switzerland was the clearing house bank for the Reich; 79 per cent of Germany's wartime gold transfers were with the Swiss National Bank and 13 per cent with the Swiss commercial banks.

In the history of the Holocaust assets and in the wider history of political neutrality the Bergier Report was a watershed. It did not move the story a great deal forward but it confirmed many of the themes which until then had been no more than theories or accusations by well placed commentators.

Less than a fortnight later, on 6 June, the second Eizenstat Report was published which both complemented and compounded the issues raised by Bergier.

This report widened the focus of historical attention beyond the strict confines of Switzerland's dealing with the Allies to include other neutral nations such as Argentina, Portugal, Spain, Sweden and Turkey. According to the report these neutral countries ran a US$7 billion trade in today's values with Nazi Germany. Nazi Germany offered looted gold and these nations sold key war materials, including iron ore and tungsten (a steel hardener) in return.

Together, the two Eizenstat reports—the first was released in May 1997—and the Bergier Report will become the template for all future discussion within the Holocaust assets debate. Hopefully they will work as references for all discussions on the duties of Switzerland, its central banks and its commerical banks. On a wider front they should also serve as a framework for debate on the role of wartime governments, commercial institutions and art galleries across Europe. Separately, they should be consulted during any renegotiation of the 1945 Washington Accord.

In Australia the tide is moving in the right direction but for many Holocaust survivors it is simply moving too slowly.

To date the Australian Government—in marked contrast to US Government authorities—is not involved in this debate and never has been. Neither the ministry responsible, Rod Kemp, the Assistant Treasurer, nor any members of the Treasury department have been active in pursuing justice for Australian citizens. More that 40 countries attended the Nazi gold conference in London in December 1997. Australia, with the tenth largest Jewish community in the world, was not represented.

There has been some good news, however. On 12 August 1998, to the surprise of many observers, not least Holocaust survivors in Australia, a global agreement was struck between the Swiss banks and Jewish restitution pressure groups in New York. This agreement, which allowed for A$2 billion to be distributed over three years represented a complete turnaround for the Swiss who had only two months earlier said that an offer of $1.2 billion was 'final'.

The deal between UBS, Credit Suisse and Jewish representative groups including the WJC was settled in the US District Court in Brooklyn. It allowed for restitution to more than 30 000 Jews around the world with claims on money deposited in Swiss banks before the outbreak of World War II. Combined with existing funds for Holocaust victims in Switzerland, such as the Special Fund for Holocaust Victims and the banking industry's Humanitarian Fund, the $2 billion global settlement goes a long way towards clearing Switzerland's dark legacy as a nation which profited from the war.

In effect the deal was an out-of-court settlement of the three most potent class actions which had been running in the United States. The Swiss National Bank and several Swiss industrial companies were also involved in the agreement. A key aspect of the settlement was the dropping of sanctions by elected officials across the United States. The primary objective of the settlement was to settle the Swiss banking industries' obligations to claimants on dormant accounts. Claimants working against non-Swiss banks, insurance companies, art galleries or property-holding authorities across Europe were not in any way covered by the settlement.

In Australia, the global agreement was greeted with guarded enthusiasm. Details of both elegibility and procedure relating to the settlement were still unclear in August 1998. As Rosenbaum explained, 'There are real positives to the deal, but I have concerns—at every stage of the process there has been the risk that the Swiss offer is a double-edged sword. It is here in this deal again.

> At the very least the settlement moves the process out of the political arena and into the courts—hopefully it will not get bogged down in the courts, because a lot of claimants are getting very old and they cannot wait much longer. I think settlement will be best for the worst cases and these are the bulk of the people we represent.

Rosenbaum believes the Australian claimants who have well-developed individual cases against the banks will be able to continue their solo quest for restitution: 'In other words, if there is another Stephen Baruch out there this agreement should not stop them.'

If the mechanics of the settlement are fair and efficient the deal should take enormous moral pressure off the Swiss banks and it will also allow the wider debate on Holocaust assets to mature. As this occurs the spotlight will pass to insurance companies which are now realising the depth of the problem they face in relation to unpaid Holocaust-era policies. Separately, property agencies within East European governments must now improve their commitment to the restitution of Holocaust-era properties through the creation of reliable bureaucratic procedures. Art galleries too, should be ready to face the inevitable onslaught of historical investigation; every major collection in the western world will be studied before this affair is laid to rest. The flurry of activity in 1998 surrounding disputed provenance at international art galleries may well represent the early stages of an issue which is set to dominate the art market in the next decade.

Meanwhile, among the cast of characters who appeared between these pages there has been some success, some hope and a lot of painful recollection. While the major players, such as Bronfman, Borer and D'Amato, continue to fight in their corner of the international stage, there is an increasing risk that minor players who were pivotal in this unfolding drama might get left behind.

This is most obvious in the case of Christoph Meili who now works as a $US 31 000 a year doorman in New York after fleeing Switzerland in the wake of a racist campaign. Meili's fifteen minutes of fame are long over. At the peak of the crisis he was offered a movie deal to tell his story. The movie remains unmade while Meili bemoans signing away his movie rights 'without getting a cent up front'. Gizella Weisshaus, a Holocast survivor who stunned the world when she led a class action against the Swiss banks in 1996, has also been overlooked. Her action was rejected by the courts in 1997.

In Australia, claimants have also reported mixed progress. Sydney-based Stephen Baruch received a settlement from the Swiss Bank Corporation and is currently exploring the possibility of property restitution in the former East Germany relating to his grandfather Salem Budzyner's extensive investment portfolio. The Kaldor family of Melbourne has received a settlement from Union Bank of Switzerland after a 50 year wrangle which would never have been settled if this affair had not hit the headlines in the last two years. Others have not been so lucky but they have reason to believe their cases may be heard and justice may be eventually achieved. Sarah Goldberger is in correspondence with Donhau Insurance of Vienna and the possibility of a settlement now exists where once she was laughed at by petty bureaucrats in the 1960s.

Siegmund Siegreich has retrieved an account statement from Dresdner Bank proving his family had dealings with the bank, and his case moves closer to conclusion. Separately his action against Assicurazioni Generali is now established. His cousin Ruth Crane is also refining her case against the Swiss banking industry and the Polish Government.

Arthur Shafir is no longer alone in his battle against Prudential Insurance; a second claimant has appeared in Melbourne and the two Polish-born claimants are now in negotiation with Prudential Insurance Australia through the offices of the AAJRC.

Erica Turek has yet to receive an adequate response from either the French or German authorities as to what happened to the Banque Des Pays and the money her father placed in it before the war. Similarly, Erica Deen's son Martin Moen has made little progress with the Dutch Government over the restitution for the losses incurred by his family during the war. Krystyna Hugon, too, waits for some sign of a formal restitution process being established by the Polish Government.

But the global agreement signed with the Swiss banks should mean that all dormant account claimants, including concentration camp survivors like Hillel Perlmutter, now have a real chance of restitution. Like thousands of claimants around the world, he is now waiting to see if the Swiss will right the wrongs of more than fifty years and distribute funds to those whose need and deserve them most.

ENDNOTES

Preface

Marrus, Michael, *The Holocaust In History*, Penguin Books, 1987.

Chapter 1

Interview with Thomas Bauer, Ernst and Young, Basel, 3 March 1998.

Chapter 2

1 Interview with author, November, October 1995.
2 Interview with author, September 1997.
3 'I think I can say in this case that the original amounts were peanuts', Robert Studer, President of United Bank of Switzerland, 23 February 1996, quoted by Reuters.
4 Kirby, James, Settling the Account, *The Weekend Australian*, 19 July 1997.
5 Ibid.
6 Interview with author, September 1997.

Chapter 3

1 Oswald Pohl, chief of the Economic Office of the SS at Nuremburg, quoted in *The Rise and Fall of the Third Reich* by William Shirer, p 974. 'The objects in question were rings, watches, eyeglasses, gold bars, wedding rings, brooches, pins, gold fillings and other valuables.'
2 Interview with author Zurich, 4 March 1998.
3 Source withheld.
4 'A war that must be won', Ambassador Carlo Jagmetti, quoted in a confidential report dated 19 December 1996 and published in Sonntagzeitung newspaper on 26 January 1997.
5 Interview with author, Melbourne, December 1997.
6 Bower, Tom, *Blood Money*, Macmillan, 1997, p 224. 'This is a thorough perversion of the terms and the intent of the accord.'

Chapter 4

1 Bartrop, Paul, Australia and the Holocaust, Australian Scholarly, 1994.
2 Ibid.
3 Rubinstein, W.D., *The Jews in Australia*, Volume 2, 1945 to the present. William Heinemann Australia. 1991.
4 Ibid.
5 Stone, Deborah, 'Schindler' Survivors', *The Sunday Age*, 23 January 1997.
6 Source withheld.

7 'This is quite a precedent in terms of normal banking practice' Paul Volcker, President of the Independent Commission at a hearing of the US House Banking Committee, 25 June 1997.

8 'We are going to see Swiss bank secrecy come tumbling down when they publish the names of 20 000 dormant Swiss bank accounts', Edgar Bronfman, WJC President, 24 July 1997, to press agencies.

9 Phone interview with author October 1997.

Chapter 6

1 Interview with author, Sydney, November 1997.

2 Interview with author, Melbourne, December 1997.

3 Harris, David, 'Begin legislation process against Generali', *Jerusalem Post*, 10 June 1997, p 4.

4 Interview with author, Melbourne, February 1998.

5 Lennon, Peter, 'Shocked survivor finds she owns part of Auschwitz'. *The Guardian*, carried in *The Sydney Morning Herald*, 24 April 1998, p 9.

Chapter 7

1 Public letter from Senator Alfonse D'Amato to Swiss Bankers Association President, Georg Krayer, 10 October 1997.

2 Interview with author, Zurich, March 1998.

3 'It pains me to put such a small price on my parents' life, but this is what my lawyer has advised me', Charles Sonabend, whose parents died in Auschwitz after being turned away at the Swiss border, speaking at a press conference 11 October 1997.

4 '(The council) deplores threats of boycotts that have been urged against Switzerland', formal statement from The World Council of Orthodox Jewish Communities, 1 December 1997.

5 Mathis Cabiallavetta, Director of United Bank of Switzerland, to press agencies, 21 November 1997.

Chapter 8

1 Lyons, John, 'Kill The Australian', *Good Weekend*, 28 December 1991, Sydney.

2 Attwood, Alan, 'Mayor in apology for city's riot shame', *The Age*, 4 April 1998, p 23, Melbourne.

3 Interview with the author, Melbourne, January 1998.

4 Interview with author, Melbourne, January 1998.

5 Operation Safehaven Report 12179, 26 July 1945.

6 Interview with author, Sydney, October 1997.

Chapter 9

1 Interview with the author, Warsaw, March 1998.
2 Interview with the author, Sydney, October 1997.

Chapter 10

1 Gill, Michael, 'The Donohoe's Side of the Story', *Australian Financial Review*, 10 March 1994, p 16.
2 Interview with author Melbourne, March 1998.

Chapter 11

1 Moen, Martin, *The Deen Years*, (unpublished family history) 1988.
2 Moen, Martin, phone interview with author November 1997.

Chapter 12

1 Interview with author, Melbourne, January 1998.
2 'We will not sit back quietly', Swiss Senator Dick Marty, speaking on Swiss national television, 19 March 1998.
3 'Taxpayers' money will not be spent in this manner', Swiss Foreign Minister Flavio Cotti, television interview 3 April 1998.

Chapter 13

1 Adam Czerniakow had been a Polish patriot and community leader in the Warsaw ghetto. In July 1942 he refused to provide any more Jews for 'resettlement in the east', knowing that the people he delivered to the Nazis were going straight to the death camps, Czerniakow took cyanide and killed himself.
2 Interview with author, May 1998.
3 Interview with author, November 1997.

Chapter 14

1 Jones, Andrea, 'Paintings Stolen, Italians Claim', *New Zealand Herald*, 4 April 1998, p 2.
2 Quote from *AAJRC Bulletin*, May 1998.
3 Interview with author, Melbourne, April 1998.
4 Lippmann, Leo, 'The Jewish Community in Hamburg in the year 1942. The liquidation of Jewish Trusts, Foundations, and organisations in Hamburg'. 1943.
5 Interview with author, Melbourne, April 1998.

SELECTED
BIBLIOGRAPHY

Bartrop, Paul. *Australia And The Holocaust*, Australian Scholarly Publishing, 1994.

Ben Sasson, H.H. *A History Of The Jewish People*, Weidenfeld And Nicolson, 1976.

Berkley, George. *Vienna And Its Jews*, ABT Books, 1988.

Bower, Tom. *Blood Money: The Swiss, the Nazis And The Looted Billions*, Macmillan Publishing Ltd, 1997.

Dwork, Deborah. *Auschwitz 1270 To The Present*, W.W.Norton and Co, 1996.

Davies, Norman. *Heart Of Europe, A Short History Of Poland*, Oxford University Press, 1984.

Eizenstat, Stuart. *US And Allied Efforts To Recover And Restore Gold And Other Assets Stolen Or Hidden By Germany During World War II*, US Department Of State, 1997.

Eizenstat, Stuart. *US And Allied Wartime And Postwar Relations And Negotiations With Argentina, Portugal, Spain, Sweden, and Turkey On Looted Gold And German External Assets And US Concerns About The Fate Of Wartime Ustasha Treasury*, US Government Printing Office, 1998.

Gilbert, Martin. *The Jews Of Europe*, Macmillan Publishing Ltd, 1984.

Gilbert, Martin. *The Boys: Triumph Over Adversity*, Weidenfeld and Nicolson, 1996.

Goldhagen, Daniel. *Hitlers Willing Executioners*, Alfred Knopf Ltd, 1996.

Hempel George, Bala Shanmugam, Craig Turton. *Bank Management*, Jacaranda Wiley Ltd, 1992.

Hilberg, Raul. *The Destruction Of The European Jews*, Holmes And Meier, 1985.

Kagan, Joram. *Poland's Jewish Heritage*, Hippocrene Books, 1992.

LeBor, Adam. *Hitlers Secret Bankers: How Switzerland Profited From Nazi Genocide*, Pocket Books, Simon and Schuster Ltd, 1997.

Marrus, Michael, *The Holocaust In History*, Penguin Books, 1987.

Marrus, Michael, Paxton Robert. *Vichy France And The Jews*, Calmann Levy Ltd, 1981.

Medding, Peter. *Jews In Australian Society*, Macmillan Publishing Ltd, 1973.

Nicholas, Lynn. *The Rape Of Europa: The Fate Of Europe's Treasures In The Third Reich And The Second World War*, Borzoi Books, Alfred Knopf Ltd, 1985.

Ostrow, Ruth. *The New Boy Network*, William Heinemann Ltd, 1987.

Rubinstein, William. *The Jews In Australia: A Thematic History, Volume 2, 1945–To The Present*, William Heinemann Ltd, 1991.

Shirer, William. *The Rise And Fall Of The Third Reich*, Secker and Warburg Ltd, 1960.

United States Holocaust Memorial Museum, *Historical Atlas Of The Holocaust*, Simon And Schuster Macmillan, 1996.
Vincent, Isabel. *Hitlers Silent Partners: Swiss Banks, Nazi Gold And The Pursuit Of Justice*, William Morrow and Company Inc, 1997.
Encylopaedia Judaica, Ketter Publishing House Jerusalem, 1972.

INDEX

209